Lead Anyway

The Truth About Grit, Growth, and Getting It Wrong First

William Long Jr

Acknowledgments

This book is for the ones who never gave up on me, especially when I gave up on myself. To my children, Jakub, Zoe, Abigail, Madeline, Vivienne, and Nathan, you are the reason I kept climbing. You gave me purpose when I felt empty, and strength when I was weak. Everything I am becoming is because of you. To my sister Erica, you have been my rock. The quiet leader of our family, your strength, steadiness, and unwavering support have carried me through more than you know. Without you, I would not be where I am today. To my mom and dad, Carolyn and Bill Sr, thank you for doing your best to provide and support me throughout my life. From coming to every football game to standing by and encouraging me at every wrestling match, your presence and love have been a foundation I could always rely on. To SFC James VanHuffel, your call changed everything. You saw something in me when I was ready to quit. You threw me a lifeline disguised as a job. I owe you more than words can repay.

To the Soldiers I've trained, led, and learned from, you are the heartbeat of this story. Every page echoes the truth I've lived: leadership is messy, but it matters.

To the quiet warriors, the single dads, the burnt-out cops, the wounded Soldiers, the silent sufferers, this is your story, too.

To my wife, Lynn.
You came into my life when I was still rebuilding, still carrying more than I could admit — and you stayed. You brought steadiness, patience, and a quiet strength I didn't know I needed. You've seen every version of me and stood beside me with grace.

Thank you for believing in me before I believed in myself, for supporting the late nights, and for giving our family a foundation of love and resilience. This book exists because you helped me find the courage to speak my truth.

And to the reader: If you've ever fallen, failed, or questioned your worth, this book is your reminder that it's never too late to get back up.

Lead anyway.

Author Disclaimer

This book is a work of nonfiction based on the author's real-life experiences. To protect the privacy of individuals and institutions referenced, certain names, locations, and identifying details have been changed or omitted. The events described are presented as accurately and truthfully as memory allows, but they reflect the author's perspective, which may differ from that of others involved.

The purpose of this book is not to assign blame or glorify hardship, but to explore personal growth through real challenges. This is a story of leadership forged in failure, redemption found in responsibility, and the quiet strength it takes to keep moving forward, even when the path isn't clear.

If you find pieces of yourself in these pages, know this: You are not alone. You are not beyond redemption. You were built for something more.

Lead anyway.

Table of Contents

Introduction:

You're Not Broken, You're Becoming

Let's get something straight from the beginning: I didn't write this book because I always got it right. I wrote it because I didn't.

I've led from anger, fear, exhaustion, and even pride. I've made decisions I regret. I've taken the wrong job, stayed too long in the wrong place, followed the wrong people, and ignored the right instincts. I've been both the hero and the villain in my own story.

And yet, I've led. Anyway.

If you picked up this book because you feel stuck, burned out, overlooked, or unqualified, you're in the right place. This book is for people who know what it feels like to carry the weight of others without always having someone to carry theirs. For people who have made hard calls and had to live with the consequences. For the ones rebuilding, again.

This isn't a TED Talk in hardback. It's a field manual. For the tired. The flawed. The ones still standing.

I've lived multiple lives: awkward teenage athlete, combat-tested Soldier, SWAT cop, recruiter, manager, husband, father, and late-blooming academic. I've sat in courtrooms and classrooms. I've worn dress blues and prison blues. Each chapter in my life came with a leadership lesson, not from books, but from failure, pressure, fatigue, and grit.

Leadership isn't about perfection. It's about presence.

If you've ever led a team, a classroom, a patrol, a shift, or a family, and questioned if you were good enough, this is for you. If you've ever fallen and still got back up, even when no one noticed, this is for you. If you've ever doubted your own worth but kept showing up anyway, this is for you.

Leadership isn't for the flawless. It's for the faithful.
Faithful to the people. Faithful to the mission.
Even when the mission is unclear, and the people are you.

So here's my promise:
This book won't pretend.
It won't polish the pain or skip the failures.
It will walk with you through what leadership really costs, and why it's still worth it.

If you're ready to lead, not because you're perfect, but because you're still willing. Then let's begin.

Lead anyway.

Chapter 1
The Quiet Provider

I didn't understand it at the time, but my first leadership lesson didn't come from a coach, a uniform, or a motivational quote. It came from a man who never once called himself a leader.

He didn't wear a rank. He didn't run meetings. He just showed up, day after day, when it was hardest, and never asked for applause.

It came from my dad.

He grew up in a Catholic orphanage in Chicago after his father died and his mother, overwhelmed and unable to cope, gave up custody. From that moment on, his life was built on survival. The stories of those years weren't passed down, but they didn't need to be. You could see the truth in the calluses on his hands, the quiet in his voice, and the way he always walked like he was carrying something heavier than anyone else could see.

When he aged out of the orphanage, he stepped into adulthood with nothing but a diploma, a plastic bag of belongings, and a work ethic forged in hardship. No money. No safety net. No backup plan. And yet, he never stopped moving forward.

He took whatever jobs he could find: bus driver, night watchman, maintenance man, fiberglass factory worker, RV assembly line laborer, and finally, plant foreman. Promotions weren't given; they were clawed out of gravel with bare hands and sore backs. He didn't talk about the grind. He lived it.

We were poor. We moved constantly. Bankruptcy came more than once. But even when everything around us felt unstable, my dad didn't waver. He drove a beat-up Oldsmobile that started with a screwdriver and rattled like a junkyard, but it got him to work every day. He worked second and third shifts, came home covered in grease or fiberglass, and often skipped meals so we could eat.

He wore the same pair of boots until they split open. He never bought anything for himself. And he never once asked for recognition.

At the time, I didn't appreciate it. I resented the instability. I wanted something more structured, more certain. But what I didn't realize then was that I had already been handed the greatest leadership lesson of my life:

Real leaders don't announce themselves. They carry the weight quietly.

He didn't lecture me about sacrifice. He lived it. He didn't tell me how to lead. He showed me, by never quitting, never complaining, and never letting his family fall apart, even when the world around him did.

He showed up. Every single day. And he gave more than he had, over and over again.

I still remember the nights he came home from third shift, eyes bloodshot, hands swollen and cracked from handling chemicals or industrial machines. He'd sit at the edge of his bed, pull off those worn boots, and not say a word. But I could feel the weight he carried even in his silence. He didn't have to speak. His life preached a sermon of sacrifice.

I didn't fully understand what he had given until years later, when I found myself doing the same, coming home in uniform, sore and spent from a 14-hour day, peeling off gear in silence, packing lunches in the dark so my kids would be ready for school the next morning. No applause. No spotlight. Just presence. And in that quiet, I realized I had become him.

He passed away in 2021, after a brutal fight with lung cancer. By then, I was old enough to understand the weight he carried and the love he showed in the only language he knew, providing, enduring, sacrificing.

We never had that big heart-to-heart. But I no longer need it.

His life was the lesson.

Leadership Debrief: Lessons from the Quiet Provider

- **Sacrifice without spotlight builds credibility.** The strongest leaders don't need recognition; they just need to be reliable.
- **Presence matters more than polish.** You don't need to be flashy, just there, every single day.
- **Consistency is more powerful than charisma.** You don't have to inspire with words when your actions speak louder.
- **Your past doesn't disqualify you.** My dad's pain didn't prevent him from leading. It prepared him.
- **You will be remembered for what you carried.** I don't remember lectures. I remember the Oldsmobile. The graveyard shifts. The silence, and the strength inside it.

You may not feel like a leader yet. Maybe life's broken you down a few times. Maybe you feel like you're barely holding it together. But if you're showing up when it's hard, carrying weight no one sees, and refusing to quit, you already are leading.

You don't have to wait for a title or a promotion. You just have to **lead anyway.**

"On June 2, 2018, my dad completed a 5K walk, just six months after having half a lung removed due to lung cancer. The finish line was inside Notre Dame Stadium. It was one of his proudest accomplishments, and rightfully so."

Chapter 2
Encyclopedias and Endurance

We didn't have much growing up. There were no big vacations, no name-brand clothes, and no safety net when things fell apart. But we had grit, imagination, and just enough chaos to learn how to navigate through noise. While other kids had video games and cable TV, I had a backyard, a few beat-up bikes, and a shelf of books that changed my life.

That shelf held a full set of encyclopedias, purchased, oddly enough, by my dad from a door-to-door salesman. For a family that couldn't always pay the electric bill, that purchase didn't make a lot of financial sense. But to me, it was gold.

I read those encyclopedias cover to cover. Not as homework, but as escape. As education. As fuel. I devoured pages on volcanoes, World War II, the Cold War, animal anatomy, foreign countries, and presidents. I didn't realize it then, but those books were laying bricks for a foundation I would build on for the rest of my life.

On the surface, buying encyclopedias may have seemed like a poor financial decision. We didn't even have reliable heat in the winter or air conditioning in the summer. But those books were more important than Nintendo, new bikes, or cable TV. They were the one purchase from my childhood that felt like an investment, not in comfort, but in possibility. And I wonder now, as a parent myself, what my mom and dad sacrificed to buy them. What bill went unpaid? What grocery list got shorter? What need did they silently push aside to make sure that knowledge lived on our bookshelf?

I wasn't the smartest kid in class, but I was the most curious. While others memorized to pass, I read to understand. I wasn't chasing a grade; I was chasing something better: the belief that learning gave me power, and discipline gave me direction.

Choosing Different, Quietly

My home life wasn't exactly a model of structure. My parents smoked. Arguments about bills echoed down the hall. My siblings picked up habits that weren't healthy. It would've been easy to follow that same path. But I didn't.

Not because I thought I was better, but because I wanted better. Better than the constant financial panic. Better than the ceiling fan spinning slowly while no one spoke. Better than the quiet sadness that hung in the air like cigarette smoke.

So I studied. I kept my head down. I said no when others said yes to easy escapes. I did my homework without being told. I wasn't trying to stand out. I was just trying not to sink.

That's when I learned something important. Leadership starts with what you do when no one's clapping.

Finding Purpose in the Grind

By high school, I knew I needed an outlet. I wasn't athletic in the natural sense, but I had heart. I joined football and wrestling, not because I was good, but because they demanded everything I had.

In football, I was a skinny wide receiver. Not the most talented, but I had speed and heart. I ran precise routes, blocked like a lineman, and never backed down from a hit. I knew I wasn't going to be the star of the team, but I refused to be a liability. I earned my spot by showing up early, staying late, and outworking the guy ahead of me.

Wrestling was even harder. My first year, I lost every match. Every single one. But I kept showing up. I kept grinding. I watched a film. I studied technique. And I slowly began to win, first a round, then a match. Not enough to call myself great, but enough to prove I wasn't done.

Those years taught me what school couldn't:

- How to lose with dignity.
- How to endure when things hurt.
- How to keep pushing when progress is invisible.

There's a quiet power in getting better when no one's watching. That's where leadership begins.

The Unseen Decisions That Shape Us

I didn't party. I didn't smoke. I didn't rebel outwardly. But that doesn't mean I wasn't making hard decisions. Every time I said no to the crowd, every time I stayed in to study, every time I walked away from trouble, I was quietly building something.

That's what most people don't understand about discipline: it's invisible at first. It doesn't announce itself. But it adds up. And over time, those decisions begin to shape who you are.

I didn't have a mentor. I didn't have a roadmap. I just had a gut feeling that if I stayed steady, if I kept learning, kept pushing, kept showing up, things would eventually break open.

And they did.

Leadership Debrief: Lessons from Encyclopedias and Endurance

- **Discipline begins in private.** The habits you build when no one is watching shape the leader you become when they are.
- **Grit is earned through losing.** Failure isn't a flaw, it's the forge where strength is built.
- **Environment isn't destiny.** You can grow up around dysfunction and still choose discipline. Leadership is a choice, not a condition.
- **Small choices matter.** Turning down the party. Opening the book. Showing up for practice. These are the quiet decisions that separate the average from the exceptional.
- **Curiosity is a superpower.** When you believe you can learn your way out of anything, you stop fearing what you don't know.

You don't have to come from perfection to become a leader. You just have to want something more and be willing to outwork the noise around you.

That's where leadership begins. You lead yourself first. And then you **lead anyway.**

Chapter 3
The Choice

By the time I reached my senior year of high school, everything felt like it was coming to a head. I had done all the right things, or at least tried to. I kept my grades up. I stayed out of trouble. I was a decent athlete. I worked jobs in the summer. From the outside, it looked like I had a clear path: college. But inside, I was torn.

I had been accepted to Wabash College, a small, all-male liberal arts school known for its academics and tradition. They gave me a decent scholarship. My parents were proud. My teachers congratulated me. My guidance counselor told me this was my ticket out. And maybe it was. But something didn't sit right.

I didn't want to just study history; I wanted to *make* it. I didn't want to debate leadership in a classroom; I wanted to *live* it, feel it, earn it. I felt a pull I couldn't explain. I was drawn to service. To something real. Something hard. Something that mattered.

The Army had been whispering to me for years. I'd watched Desert Storm on TV as a kid. I looked up to Soldiers, not because they were cool, but because they were committed. They had purpose. They sacrificed. And I wanted that kind of gravity in my life.

Still, I chose college. I told myself it was the smart move. I could always join later. I could do both. But the truth was, I didn't want to disappoint anyone. I was trying to be what everyone expected of me. And that choice, though logical, felt like a betrayal of something inside me.

I enrolled at Wabash and moved onto campus. It was everything it promised to be, tight-knit, intellectual, steeped in tradition. I joined a fraternity. I played football. I studied psychology and history. I wrote papers. I made friends. But I also drifted.

Classes didn't light me up the way I'd hoped. Parties didn't fulfill me the way they seemed to for others. I wasn't lost, I was *misaligned.* I kept asking myself: *Is this it?* Is this what success is supposed to feel like? Because all I felt was restless.

And then one night, everything changed.

I saw a television commercial for the U.S. Army. Nothing flashy. Just a Soldier walking with purpose, a voice-over talking about challenge and growth, and a tagline that hit deeper than I expected. It didn't inspire me, it *convinced* me. I wasn't chasing anything. I was coasting, waiting, hoping life would show up and give me purpose.

I shut the TV off and sat in silence. It felt like I was staring at a fork in the road, one side was comfort, the other was challenge. I already knew which way I was going.

The very next day, my roommate and I got in the car and drove to Indianapolis. It was quiet at first; neither of us really knew what to expect. Then he asked, "You really serious about this?" I remember looking at him and saying, "More than anything." It was the first time in months I felt that kind of clarity. I wasn't second-guessing. I wasn't trying to talk myself into it. I was just *ready.*

The recruiting office was tucked into a strip mall. Fluorescent lights, old posters on the wall, the faint smell of coffee and printer ink, it was a world away from the Wabash lecture halls. And yet, it felt more real. More grounded. The recruiter looked up as we walked in. He didn't try to sell me anything. He asked what I was looking for.

"Infantry," I said without hesitation.

He gave me a polite but firm shake of the head. "Not in the Reserves."

Before I could be disappointed, my roommate chimed in: "What about Military Police?"

I paused, then nodded. It didn't matter. I didn't need the perfect MOS; I needed a *way in.* A mission. A direction. The recruiter handed me an application, not a contract- and I filled it out right there on the spot. No hesitation. I was done waiting. Done pretending I was content.

Two weeks later, we went to MEPS. I remember the bus ride, the sterile hallways, the sense that something serious was happening. On February 13, 1996, I officially joined the Army Reserve.

Telling my parents was nerve-wracking. I didn't know how they'd respond. But when I told them, there wasn't anger, just concern. And behind that, a flicker of pride. They didn't fully understand why I needed this, but they respected that I did.

I would finish my sophomore year at Wabash before shipping off to basic training. But my heart had already left campus. I went to class. I did the work. But I no longer felt tied to the traditional path. I had chosen something harder. Something more uncertain. But something that, for the first time, felt like *mine.*

The Courage to Course-Correct

People don't talk enough about the bravery it takes to change direction, to walk away from a path everyone else approves of in order to chase something only you understand.

But leadership isn't about always getting it right the first time. It's about owning your choices, even when they're uncomfortable. It's about admitting when the life you're building doesn't match the person you're becoming.

That decision, to leave college, to enlist, to trust my gut, wasn't easy. But it was necessary. And it taught me something I've carried ever since:

You don't find your purpose by pretending to be someone else. You find it by listening to the voice that won't shut up, even when the world is applauding your silence.

Leadership Debrief: Lessons from The Choice

- **Success isn't alignment.** Just because you're winning by someone else's scoreboard doesn't mean you're playing the right game.

- **Misalignment feels like restlessness.** Pay attention to it. It's not a weakness; it's your instincts trying to save you.
- **Quiet desires matter.** You don't have to justify your dreams to people who weren't built to carry them.
- **Course correction is leadership.** The ability to pivot with honesty is more powerful than pretending with consistency.
- **Lead yourself by trusting yourself.** No one knows your calling as you do. And no one can walk your path but you.

You'll be praised for playing it safe. But you'll only feel alive when you take the leap.

Lead anyway.

Chapter 4
Fraternity and Fog

After I enlisted, everything looked the same, but nothing felt the same.

I finished out my sophomore year at Wabash, but the energy I once tried to summon for classes and campus life had faded. I was still going through the motions, turning in papers, suiting up for rugby, attending fraternity events, but mentally, I was already on a different path. I had seen the other road. I had chosen it. And now everything around me felt… temporary.

Wabash was still a good school, and my friends were still good guys. But I started to feel like a ghost in the house. I had one foot in this world and one foot in another. And the more I drifted between the two, the more I saw how lost I had been. Before the Army, I had been treading water, playing the game, following the script. Now, with basic training on the horizon, I was swimming toward something. Something solid. Something mine.

The parties got old fast. I'd go, maybe have a drink, nod along to the noise, but I wasn't really there. I wasn't judging the others for enjoying it. I just knew it wasn't for me anymore. I wasn't chasing validation. I wasn't chasing numbness. I was chasing clarity, strength, direction. And all of that felt lightyears away from keg stands and hangovers.

Oddly enough, rugby was the one thing that still lit a fire in me. It was aggressive, disciplined, and demanded toughness. Unlike football, rugby didn't rely on stars; it relied on grit. I wasn't the biggest guy on the field, but I had endurance, timing, and just enough ferocity to be respected. When I played, I could forget the noise. I could feel sharp again.

But even that had a shelf life. I was evolving. I wanted to grow, not coast. I wasn't content being good at something that no longer aligned with who I was becoming.

Somewhere during that semester, I drove back to the recruiter's office to confirm my ship date. Everyone around me couldn't believe it. *Look at what you're giving up,* they said. Wabash graduates went on to become successful lawyers, executives, and doctors. I was walking away from a future that most people saw as plush and predictable. They saw opportunity in offices and boardrooms. I saw it in dirt and blood. They couldn't understand, but I did.

When I first arrived at Wabash, I was filled with excitement. I was socially quiet, unsure of myself in a sea of bold personalities, but I was stepping into a new life. I joined a fraternity, not because I needed a place to party, but because I needed a place to belong. For a time, it filled that gap. But now, I was filling it with something stronger: purpose.

That visit to the recruiting office wasn't just about logistics; it was about reassurance. I needed to see the next chapter in writing. I needed to know that this version of me wasn't just a dream, that I had already stepped across the line.

As that semester drew to a close, I felt something I hadn't felt in a long time: momentum.

I wasn't just existing anymore. I was *becoming.*

I wasn't pretending to care about things that didn't fit.

I was building something, even if I couldn't fully explain what that was yet. I still remember the last few nights before I left for basic. The house was loud with end-of-year parties, laughter, and traditions. I stood on the porch one night, looking out at the quiet street. And I realized, I wasn't afraid.

I was ready.

The Power of Misalignment

Sometimes the clearest sign of growth isn't a big win—it's the discomfort of misalignment. When what used to feel right now feels empty, don't ignore it. That tension is sacred. It's telling you to move.

Fraternity taught me about brotherhood. College taught me about thinking. But neither could teach me who I was. Only action could do that. Only service. Only trial.

And so I chose the fog over the familiar. I walked into the unknown because I trusted the pull more than the praise.

Leadership Debrief: Lessons from Fraternity and Fog

- **Growth isn't loud.** Sometimes it looks like stepping back from what used to excite you.
- **You don't have to stay loyal to an outdated version of yourself.** Evolution isn't betrayal, it's maturity.
- **Grit shows up in how you prepare, not just how you perform.**
- **Readiness is a feeling.** When it's time to move, you'll know.

You'll be tempted to delay the leap until everything feels perfect. But becoming who you're meant to be rarely happens on a schedule.

Lead anyway.

Chapter 5
The Barracks and the Burden

Basic training at Fort McClellan didn't just change me, it exposed me.

When I arrived in Alabama in the heat of summer, I was surrounded by strangers, stripped of comfort, and submerged in a world where identity was broken down to be rebuilt. There were no accolades, no past achievements to cling to, just uniforms, discipline, and a relentless cadence of orders. That's exactly what I wanted. I wasn't looking for comfort, I was looking for transformation.

The first day of training is burned into my memory. It was a bright, hot day. We traveled from reception to the training area, packed into buses, each of us weighed down with two massive duffel bags and the only luggage we were allowed to carry, the gear that would get us through the next 20 weeks. As the buses rolled to a stop, chaos exploded. Drill Sergeants descended in a fury. The infamous "shark attack" had begun.

People were screaming, crying, and puking as we were made to pick up our bags, drop them, pick them up again, over and over until our arms gave out and our minds went numb. Pushups, flutter kicks, mountain climbers, everywhere you looked, someone was getting smoked. And right there, in the middle of the madness, I remember thinking: *I have arrived.*
It sounds strange, but I didn't want to be anywhere else.

I wasn't alone. My college roommate had enlisted with me. We were in the same platoon, which gave me a strange sense of familiarity in the chaos. But that comfort was tested. As training wore on, my battle buddy, someone I had taken it upon myself to help, started to slow us down. My roommate pulled me aside one day and said, "Leave him. He's making us all look bad, and we're paying for his mistakes."

I understood the frustration, but I couldn't follow that advice. That isn't what leaders do. You don't discard people because they're inconvenient. Leadership means taking the hit with them, not tossing them aside to save face. My roommate wasn't wrong about the cost. But I wasn't about to pay it by sacrificing someone else.

I thrived in the structure. The physical demands were high, but I had prepared. I wasn't the strongest, but I was fast, focused, and driven. I volunteered for everything. Extra PT? I was in. Fire watch? No problem. "Smoke sessions"? I embraced them. I wanted to prove, to myself and to everyone else, that I belonged here.

It didn't take long for the drill sergeants to notice. I wasn't the loudest or the cockiest, but I was always ready. I wasn't trying to win attention. I was chasing respect.

Basic training was more than physical. It stripped away everything superficial, status, style, even our names. We weren't "Long" or "Martinez" or "Smith" anymore; we were "Private." We learned how to march before we ran, how to shut up and listen, how to follow before leading. Even the cadence songs and drills were designed to synchronize us into one unit, one rhythm. Individuality wasn't the point; identity through discipline was.

The days bled together in sweat and dust. We woke up before the sun and ended each day sore and spent. But somewhere in the grind, I found clarity. There's something pure about being reduced to your will and your effort. No one cared about your backstory. They only cared if you showed up and gave everything.

We learned fast that failure didn't mean you were done; it meant you had more to learn. We were taught to encourage the weak and challenge the strong. When one of us fell behind, we circled back. That wasn't written in a rulebook, it was baked into the ethos. *No one gets left behind.* Not in the Army. Not in life.

The rifle range taught us precision under pressure. Gas chamber training taught us control under chaos. And obstacle courses? They taught us how to fall, get up, and run again, faster. Nothing came easy, and that was the point.

Then came the moment that shaped my definition of leadership.

One of my battle buddies was struggling, physically, emotionally, and mentally. The kind of guy most would write off as a weak link. But something inside me wouldn't let that happen. I took time after lights out to help him square away his gear. I talked to him during chow and drill. I gave him pointers, motivated him when he wanted to quit, and sometimes just stood next to him so he didn't feel alone. He didn't ask for a savior, just a brother who wouldn't let him fall behind.

Helping him made my own training harder. I could've breezed through, stayed in my lane, and looked good doing it. But that wasn't why I was here. If the Army was going to forge leaders, then this was the forge. Leadership, I realized, wasn't about rising above others. It was about lifting others up, even when no one's watching.

It was also in those moments, sweaty, angry, exhausted- that I started learning what real endurance meant. Not just physical endurance, but emotional endurance. The kind of grit to push someone else's burden along with your own. That would serve me in every chapter that followed.

The most brutal day of training came toward the end, the ruck march. Miles under weight. Feet blistered, shoulders burning, calves seizing. Every step was a test. And yet, I remember looking around and seeing others struggling worse than I. So I adjusted my pace, offered a hand, even carried an extra canteen. It slowed me down. But it proved something deeper:

I could suffer without making it about me.

That march didn't break me. It baptized me. And I walked off that field knowing I wasn't just built to survive. I was built to serve.

I didn't see it then, but that moment would shape the rest of my military career and my life.

The First Test of Character

Basic training is designed to break you. But sometimes, what emerges from the pressure isn't just a tougher version of you, it's a clearer one.

I walked into Fort McClellan with a chip on my shoulder and something to prove.

I walked out with something better: a foundation.

A deeper understanding of selfless service.

A fire lit not by ego, but by commitment.

It was there, in that uniform and under that pressure, that I began to shed the boy I had been and started becoming the man I wanted to be.

Leadership Debrief: Lessons from the Forge

- **Volunteering isn't about ego, it's about exposure to growth.**
- **Great leaders aren't the fastest; they're the ones who don't leave others behind.**
- **Your first true test won't come with a spotlight; it'll come when no one's watching.**
- **Helping someone else succeed will cost you comfort, but it builds character.**
- **Discipline is the great equalizer; earn respect with effort, not noise.**
- **True grit isn't loud, it's consistent.**
- **Suffering isn't weakness. It's training. Especially when you choose to suffer for someone else.**
- **You'll be pressured to abandon others to get ahead. Real leaders hold the line.**

True leadership doesn't start with a title. It starts the moment you choose to carry someone else's weight when you don't have to.

Lead anyway.

Chapter 6
The Return to Wabash

I came home from basic training a different person.

The transformation was more than physical; it was mental, emotional, and spiritual. I had been broken down and rebuilt. I had discovered what it meant to lead, to serve, and to sacrifice.

But none of that prepared me for the disorientation I felt stepping back into the world I had left behind.

Wabash hadn't changed. But I had. I was no longer impressed by the prestige or the parties. The halls that once represented possibility now echoed with emptiness. I had been chasing someone else's idea of success, fancy job titles, law degrees, and six-figure salaries. And now, it all felt hollow.

When I first arrived at Wabash as a freshman, I was quiet but hopeful. I joined a fraternity not because I needed it, but because I wanted to belong. I wanted a connection. Brotherhood. At the time, it seemed like the best way to find it. I immersed myself in college life, football, parties, and long nights of studying, broken up by longer nights of drinking. I was finding my footing.

But now I walked those same paths with new eyes. I didn't feel like a college kid anymore. I had stood in formation at 4 a.m. I had rucked through Alabama heat with blood in my boots. I had learned how to suffer without quitting and how to lead without recognition. Wabash felt like the past.

Everyone was excited I was back, at least, on the surface. But underneath their smiles was confusion. *Why would someone leave Wabash to become a soldier? Didn't I know what I was giving up?* People who graduated from here became lawyers, doctors, and CEOs. And yet, I had walked away from all of it, for dirt and blood and discipline.

They didn't understand. But I did.

The Army hadn't taken anything from me. It had given me clarity. For the first time, I knew what I wanted: purpose. Direction. Something real.

Before I go further, let me introduce Shelby, because this is the first time her name appears on these pages.

I met her in the spring of my freshman year on an online forum. After chatting for a few weeks, I drove up to Michigan State University for a weekend cookout she invited me to. Shelby was smart, grounded, and, unlike most college students we knew, already a mom to a little boy named AJ. Her maturity drew me in; her calm steadiness balanced my restlessness.

We spent long weekends driving back and forth between Wabash and Lansing, talking about ambition, responsibility, and what it means to build a life while everyone else was busy building résumés. She was my first real girlfriend. And in that season of confusion, she felt like an anchor.

The realization came during the ride back from Fort McClellan to Wabash College after graduation. My parents and Shelby had driven down for the ceremony, and I rode back with them. Sitting in the back seat, staring out the window as miles of highway slipped by, I knew with quiet certainty that something had changed. Shelby was talking to my mom about plans for the fall semester, but I was somewhere else entirely.
I realized I wasn't returning to the life they expected me to have; I was returning to end it.

Everything about our relationship felt different. The distance I had once felt from my purpose was now the distance I felt in our connection. She had supported me in her own way. But I had changed. And what I needed now wasn't support, it was freedom. Freedom to grow. Freedom to fail. Freedom to live a life I chose.

I broke up with Shelby not long after. She was hurt that I made the decision on my own, but I had made peace with it.

I wasn't looking for permission anymore.

I was chasing who I was meant to be. It wasn't an impulsive decision. I wrestled with it for weeks. But every time I sat in class or walked through campus, I felt a growing sense of disconnection.

It wasn't just about Shelby. It was about *everything.*

The future I once imagined, a house, a degree, a steady job, felt like someone else's script. Not mine.

I finished out the semester. I did my work. I showed up. But the fire was gone. My heart wasn't there anymore.

I didn't belong in classrooms that taught theory while I had lived reality. I didn't want to pretend. I didn't want to delay. I wanted to serve.

Sometimes I would sit in the library, surrounded by classmates buried in textbooks, and feel like I was a ghost haunting my own life. They were planning for futures I no longer wanted.

They were excited about internships, grad schools, and starting salaries. I was thinking about discipline, sacrifice, and service.

We were speaking different languages.

Even my fraternity brothers noticed the change. I wasn't the same guy who had rushed the house. I didn't care about the parties, the inside jokes, or the politics of who would be president next year. I had changed, and that made them uncomfortable.

A few of them asked if I was okay. I told them I was fine. But *fine* is what people say when they're trying not to set the house on fire.

I had spent years trying to fit into a mold: a good student. A college man. A future professional. But basic training had smashed that mold and revealed someone new underneath. Someone who didn't need to chase titles to feel worthy.

Someone who found more meaning in hardship than in honor roll certificates.

My professors were supportive in that polite, academic way.

They encouraged me to stay. Told me I had potential. One even offered to write a letter of recommendation if I changed my mind.

But potential without purpose is just pressure. And I was done living under other people's expectations.

By the time the semester ended, my mind was made up.

I was leaving Wabash.

I packed my things, said a few goodbyes, and didn't look back. No fanfare. No regrets.

I wasn't walking away from a future. I was walking toward one.

What came next wasn't easy. But it was mine.

Leadership Debrief: Lessons from the Fork in the Road

- **Growth often creates distance, from places, from people, from old plans.**
- **You don't have to explain your purpose to everyone.** Most won't understand, and that's okay.
- **It's not selfish to choose a different path.** It's self-respect.
- **Belonging isn't about fitting in.** It's about aligning with what feels real.
- **Breaking up isn't always about the other person.** Sometimes it's about finally choosing yourself.
- **Clarity is costly, but worth everything.**

Leaving college didn't make me a failure.
It made me honest.

Lead anyway.

Chapter 7
New Beginnings and Uncharted Roads

After leaving Wabash, I moved back home.

It felt strange returning to my old room, the same four walls that had once held a kid with vague dreams. But I wasn't that kid anymore. I was changed, physically, mentally, and emotionally. While others saw my decision as a step backward, for me, it was the first time I felt like I was standing on solid ground.

Home was both comfort and discomfort. I appreciated being around my family, but I could sense the unspoken questions in their eyes. *Was this just a phase? Were you going to finish school? What now?* I didn't have answers. What I had was a gnawing need to do something that mattered.

I bounced between jobs, doing what I could to stay busy. I started working at a local pet store, cleaning cages and stocking shelves. From there, I moved on to driving an armored car, a job that felt slightly more aligned with the structure and responsibility I had grown to appreciate. Eventually, I landed a position at the county's juvenile detention center. It was challenging work, emotionally and mentally, but it gave me a sense of purpose I hadn't felt in a while. Every day was a step away from the classroom and a step toward something I couldn't yet name.

And then I met Karen.

Karen wasn't like anyone I'd met before. We were introduced by a mutual friend who thought we might click. She had a quiet strength about her, confident without being loud, grounded without being stubborn. We started spending time together, and it didn't take long before I was drawn in. She understood my drive, my intensity, and she didn't flinch when I talked about military service or leaving behind college life. That mattered more than she probably knew.

We weren't together long before we found out she was pregnant.

I wish I could say I handled it with perfect grace and maturity. The truth is, I was scared. I was 22 years old. I didn't have a stable job, a college degree, or a five-year plan. I had grit. I had a sense of responsibility. But no road map. And yet, I knew this was a road I had to take.

Karen and I got married in 1998, and that year we welcomed our son, Jakub, into the world. Holding him for the first time rewired something in me. I didn't feel ready, but I felt resolved. I would figure it out. I would show up. I would lead.

Becoming a father didn't simplify my life; it complicated it. There were bills, tension, doubts, and moments I thought I was failing. But there was also a purpose. Real, gritty, no-days-off purpose.

I wasn't just living for myself anymore. For the first time, I understood the stakes. I was no longer chasing some abstract idea of manhood; I was building it, brick by uncertain brick. And in that messy construction site of life, I found my footing.

Some of my old friends from Wabash reached out occasionally. They were finishing degrees, landing internships, and getting accepted into law school. I was changing diapers, learning how to stretch a dollar, and working every odd job I could find. And yet, I didn't envy them. I didn't regret anything. I was building something different.

The weight of responsibility can crush you, or it can forge you. For me, it did a little of both.

There were nights Karen and I would fight about money, schedules, or the thousand small stresses that come with young marriage. We were two people trying to figure out life with a baby in our arms and dreams in our pockets. It wasn't easy. But it was *ours.*

I learned a lot in those early years of marriage. I learned how to problem-solve on a budget, how to apologize even when I didn't feel like it, and how to compromise when both of us were exhausted. I learned that leadership at home meant consistency, not control. It meant sacrifice, not speeches.

Despite the day-to-day struggles, I kept my eye on service. Just a year later, that call came, in an unexpected way.

In July 1999, I deployed with my Reserve unit to Guatemala as part of a humanitarian relief mission following Hurricane Mitch. We weren't there to fight; we were there to help. And that changed everything.

I found myself rebuilding roads, distributing aid, and working alongside locals whose lives had been shattered. There were no headlines, no glory, just sweat, humility, and service. And for the first time since returning from training, I felt alive in that old familiar way again.

That mission confirmed what I already suspected: I didn't just *want* to serve, I *needed* to. I wasn't built for sidelines or safety nets. I was built for a purpose.

The days in Guatemala were long, hot, and humbling. I saw children with nothing smiling with everything. I saw how leadership could mean lending your strength without needing to take credit. That mission etched a permanent reminder on my soul: Service is about showing up where you're needed most, not where it's most comfortable.

I still felt the tug of the Army, the pull toward structure and mission. That feeling only intensified after Guatemala.

I realized I didn't just want to serve part-time, I needed to be full-time. I needed the mission, the sense of purpose, and the camaraderie that came with active duty. It wasn't about escaping my responsibilities at home; it was about *becoming* the kind of man, father, and leader who could shoulder them.

That decision began to take root in my heart, even before the opportunity formally presented itself. After Guatemala, I knew I needed to go full-time. I submitted a formal request to transition to active duty, but it was being slow-walked through the system, going nowhere for months.

So for now, I was learning how to be a husband.
How to be a father.
How to be a man who didn't run when things got hard.

That season shaped me in ways college never could. It taught me the value of presence. It taught me how to lead without rank and love without condition. I learned that growth wasn't linear; it zigzagged through failure, doubt, and second chances.

Even though the road ahead was unclear, I knew two things: I wasn't done serving. And I hadn't even scratched the surface of who I could become.

Leadership Debrief: Lessons from Young Adulthood

- **Life doesn't wait for you to feel ready.** Show up anyway.
- **Responsibility reveals who you are, not who you say you are.**
- **You don't need a perfect plan.** You need commitment.
- **Hardship can break you, or build you.** The difference is choice.
- **Your path won't look like anyone else's,** and that's the point.
- **The most valuable leadership lessons are often learned in your own home.**
- **Sometimes, the only way forward is through.**

The moment you stop looking for the easy road is the moment you start growing.

Lead anyway.

Army Reserve deployment to Guatemala for Hurricane Mitch relief. This humanitarian mission pushed long to go on active duty.

Chapter 8
Letters to Power

It's strange how moments that seem small at first can become turning points in your life. A conversation. A sentence. A choice. Something clicks, and you realize you're done waiting. That's what writing the letter felt like.

After Guatemala, I came home with a fire burning in my chest. I had seen the impact I could make. I had seen what real service looked like. I didn't want to live halfway anymore. I wanted to be all in. Full-time Army. Not weekend drills and paperwork, I wanted a uniform on my back and a mission in my heart every day. But no matter how many times I followed the formal channels, nothing moved. My request to go on active duty was stuck in the system, passed from desk to desk with no traction.

Months went by, and I kept hearing the same thing: **"Be patient."**

Patience is a virtue. But it's not a strategy. I remember sitting at my kitchen table late one night. Karen was asleep in the other room. Jakub snored softly in his crib. The house was quiet. I was restless. Frustrated. I had followed the rules. I had done everything I was supposed to. And yet, the dream was just out of reach.

So I did something people don't usually do. I wrote a letter to the White House. Not an email. Not a form submission. A real letter. Pen and paper. Addressed to the President of the United States.

I laid it all out: my story, my service, my desire to do more, the delays I faced. I wasn't angry. I was honest. I just wanted someone, anyone, to care enough to help me serve.

I didn't expect anything to come from it. Honestly, I thought it might end up in a pile somewhere, unread and forgotten. But I needed to try. Because I couldn't stomach the idea of telling my son one day that I gave up just because things got hard.

Weeks passed.

Then one afternoon, an envelope arrived. It had the seal.

I held it in my hands, unsure if I should open it. When I finally did, it was short, polite, and official. The White House had received my letter. And they had contacted the Department of the Army.

Suddenly, doors that had been closed were opening.

I was told to resubmit my request to go full-time, and this time, it went through. No delays. No lost paperwork. It was happening.

I was going on active duty.

I remember standing in the MEPS building again, heart pounding like it was my first enlistment. I had walked into that building years earlier as a college kid chasing a new identity. Now I was a husband, a father, a man on a mission.

There was one more thing I wanted.

I didn't want just any assignment; I wanted Ft. Bragg. I wanted Airborne. I walked up to the MEPS counselor and made my case. He looked at me with a smirk and said, "You can't go to Ft. Bragg. You're not Airborne."

Without hesitation, I replied, "Then send me to Airborne."

He laughed like I was joking, but I wasn't. I was dead serious.

He must've seen something in my eyes, or maybe he just admired the boldness, because he shrugged and tapped a few keys.

"Alright," he said. "503rd Military Police Battalion at Ft. Bragg. Airborne school to follow once you're settled in."

It wasn't guaranteed. Nothing in the Army ever is.
But it was a start. And it was everything I had asked for.

Within a few weeks, my orders came through.
I was headed to Ft Bragg. Airborne.

The day those papers hit my hands, I felt like I was breathing for the first time in months. Everything I'd fought for, everything I'd written, was becoming real.

The letter hadn't just moved paperwork. It had moved my life.

I think about that moment often. Not because I think everyone should write the President to get what they want, but because it reminded me that leadership doesn't always mean waiting your turn.

Sometimes, it means taking the shot, even if no one else believes you'll make it.

Karen didn't fully understand what was driving me, but she supported me. That mattered.

When I told her I had written the President, she looked at me like I was crazy—
But then she saw the conviction in my eyes.

She didn't argue. She didn't question my motives. She just said,

"If this is what you need to do, then do it."

That moment sticks with me. Not because she agreed, but because she trusted me enough to let me chase something bigger.

That kind of support is rare. And I'll always be grateful for it.

We packed up what little we had, said goodbye to family, and moved to North Carolina. Just like that, a new chapter began.

Arriving at Ft Bragg was surreal.

The post was massive, alive with movement and energy. Soldiers marched. Helicopters buzzed overhead. The hum of something greater than yourself was everywhere.

I wasn't an outsider anymore. I was in.

I was assigned to the 108th Military Police Company (Airborne/Air Assault), which was just returning from a deployment to Kosovo. The unit was in the process of resetting, reestablishing routines, and preparing for whatever came next.

I was the new guy. No ceremony. No special welcome. Just uniforms, schedules, and the expectation that you'd keep up.

Those first few months were an adjustment. I was learning new names, new SOPs, new rhythms. But even in the middle of the learning curve, I felt something I hadn't felt in a long time: Belonging.

The early days were a blur of in-processing, briefings, and PT. I still remember the looks some of the younger Soldiers gave me. I was the guy who left college and came back. The older one. The dad.

But I didn't let that slow me down. If anything, it fueled me.

I showed up early. I stayed late. I pushed myself in every ruck, every run, every jump. I wasn't the strongest or the fastest, but I refused to be outworked. And slowly, people started to notice.

Life was hard. The pace. The standards. The constant demand to be better. It would chew you up if you weren't ready. But I was ready. I had spent the last few years preparing for this moment without even realizing it.

Every job.

Every diaper change

Every sleepless night.

It had all made me tougher. More focused. More committed.

And now, I was exactly where I was supposed to be.

I sometimes wonder what would've happened if I had never written that letter. Would I still be bouncing between jobs?
Still trying to convince someone I had more to give?

Maybe.

But that's not how my story went. Because I took the shot. I believed my voice mattered. And someone, somewhere, listened.

I share this not to sound like a hero. I share it to remind you:

Sometimes leadership means breaking the mold. It means pushing through the "no's" until you reach the "yes." It means betting on yourself, even when no one else will.

That letter wasn't about politics. It wasn't about pulling strings.

It was about refusing to let red tape decide my future. If you believe in something enough to fight for it. Write the damn letter.

Leadership Debrief: Lessons from a Letter

- **Closed doors aren't always locked; sometimes you just need to knock louder.**
- **Systems fail people. Your voice can still break through.**
- **Taking initiative is risky. So is doing nothing.**
- **Support doesn't always mean understanding. Sometimes it just means standing by.**
- **Leadership isn't a title, it's action in the face of silence.**
- **Being underestimated can be fuel. Let it burn.**
- **Persistence will outlast resistance if you don't quit.**
- **Sometimes leadership isn't about being in charge.**
- **Sometimes it's about refusing to wait.**

Lead anyway.

Chapter 9
Before the Smoke

Ft Bragg was everything I hoped it would be. Big, loud, fast-paced, exactly the kind of environment I'd craved during the years of waiting. I was finally among full-time Soldiers who lived, breathed, and bled military service.

There was no clock to punch, no second job to report to. This was it. I settled into the 108th Military Police Company (Airborne/Air Assault). While they were still coming off a deployment to Kosovo, the unit was already shifting focus. There was a current in the air, like we were being pulled toward something we couldn't see yet.

I earned my Airborne wings that spring. The jumps were exhilarating, controlled chaos that demanded focus, courage, and trust in your training. Every time I stepped out that door, I felt more alive. There was power in conquering the instinct to hold back. The ground never felt more real than after a clean PLF.

Just days before graduation, Karen told me she was pregnant.
I was going to be a dad again.

The news hit me like a thunderclap, not with fear, but with the weight of purpose. Another life would depend on me. Another reason to make this path work. There was joy and anxiety in equal measure. It reminded me that even in the chaos of military life, our personal lives continue to write their own chapters.

The rhythms of military life were finally becoming second nature. I was no longer the new guy fumbling through formations or figuring out which sergeants to avoid. I knew the routines, the personalities, the expectations.
I knew where to be, what to do, and how to get it done.

That confidence, earned through repetition, failure, and persistence, built slowly but surely.

And then came the strange briefing in July.

We were preparing to support the Pope Air Force Base open house when we were pulled aside and given a cryptic message: Be on the lookout for a white minivan. Enterprise rental. Several Arab men from Florida.

It seemed oddly specific, and oddly vague. A potential threat, but with no context. We chalked it up to intel paranoia. We logged it, filed it mentally under "unlikely," and moved on. In hindsight, it was a whisper before the scream.

Then came the scream.

September 11, 2001.

I had just come off night shift. 0700. I returned to our small house off-post. Karen had *Good Morning America* on.

She looked pale. Distracted.

"A plane hit the World Trade Center," she said.

I dried off from the shower, walked to the living room, and stood there. The news was replaying the footage. A smoking tower. Sirens. Anchors fumbling for words.

It looked like an accident. Then the second plane hit.

That was no accident. That was a message.

Time stopped. The breath left the room.

It was the silence before war.

I didn't finish my breakfast. I threw on my uniform and drove back to the post.

The traffic had frozen. The gates were jammed. Barricades. Armed guards. Flashing lights. Everyone looked like they'd been punched in the face.

As I sat in the traffic, my mind raced:

What does this mean for us?

Were we next?

Would there be more attacks?

Could we protect our families?

The line of cars barely moved, but the anxiety inside me surged forward. My knuckles were white on the steering wheel. I remember gripping it so tightly my hands hurt afterward.

Radios buzzed. Soldiers sat in silence. No music. No jokes. Just the deep hum of anticipation. By noon, everything changed.

Force protection drills. Communications lockdowns. Armed Soldiers on every corner.

The questions stopped.

We all knew**:** we were going to war. The memory of that July briefing came rushing back. The white minivan. Arab men. Florida. That wasn't paranoia. That was intelligence we didn't understand in time.

The attacks solidified everything. This wasn't peacekeeping. This was the next war. And it was coming fast.

Zoe was born on October 9. Beautiful. Healthy. Perfect.

But I held her with dread.

I wasn't afraid of fatherhood; I already had Jakub. But this was different.

I knew this time, I'd miss everything. The first steps, the first words, the birthdays.
I'd be a picture in a frame.
A voice on a recording.

I held her tighter than I probably should have.

I whispered to her in the dark. I made promises I hoped I could keep.

I told her I'd come back. I told myself I'd come back *whole.*

But deep down, I knew, War doesn't send you back the same. If it sends you back at all.

Karen and I tried to hold it together. She was postpartum and scared. I was training harder, staying longer, getting my kit ready, triple-checking my will. We were both unraveling, but too stubborn to say it.

At first, it was little things. Dishes undone. Laundry piling up.

Short words and long silences.

Then it turned into late-night arguments, about what we'd do if I didn't come home. About money. About the kids. About what neither of us wanted to say: We were both drowning.

I wanted to fix everything. She wanted me present.

But my head was already downrange.

Every time I kissed Zoe goodnight, I wondered if I was imprinting a memory she wouldn't remember. Jakub started acting out at preschool. He didn't know how to say,

"I'm scared Dad's leaving."

So he just got angry. Zoe would fall asleep on my chest while I studied maps of Afghanistan. Jakub would ask questions I couldn't answer.

He knew something was happening, even at his young age.
There's a moment you realize your kids are watching how you handle the hard stuff. I was being watched.

One night I stood in our tiny living room, holding Zoe. Jakub asleep in the next room. Karen quiet on the couch.
And I knew: I was already somewhere else.

My body was here.
But my mind was in a desert halfway around the world.

I didn't know what was coming next.
But I knew we were going to bleed.

And still I didn't want to be anywhere else.

Leadership Debrief: Smoke on the Horizon

- **You won't always see the moment coming.** Prepare anyway.
- **Leaders don't choose their timing—they rise to it.**
- **Family doesn't pause for war.** The two must coexist.
- **Mission failure can happen off the battlefield, too.** And recovery is still leadership.
- **The fog of war isn't always outside.** It's in your mind, your heart.
- **You're still leading when you're holding your daughter at 3 a.m. in a dark apartment.**
- **What you survive teaches you more than what you conquer.**

SPC William Long with Jakub during the summer of 2001 at Ft Bragg, NC

Chapter 10
The Enemy at the Gate

I deployed to Kandahar, Afghanistan, in November 2001.The air was dry and bitter, the kind that cracks your skin and burns your lungs. We flew in on C-17s under blackout conditions, stepping into a war zone that barely had infrastructure, let alone certainty. The tarmac at Kandahar Airfield was still littered with Soviet wreckage\, twisted metal, and ghost tanks from another era's failed invasion. But this was our war now.

We were among the first conventional forces on the ground, supporting early operations and establishing control in the region. There were no real barracks, no showers, no chow halls, just canvas tents, Hesco barriers, and dust. Everything was dust.

I was assigned to detainee operations, helping process suspected Taliban and Al Qaeda fighters. We built holding facilities out of plywood and concertina wire and guarded them 24/7.

We lived an austere life. Supplies were limited. We shared our MREs with detainees. Each of us was issued just two MREs a day and two liters of bottled water. At first, restrooms were nothing more than trenches dug into the earth. Trash was burned in open pits soaked with JP8 fuel. The smell clung to everything: our clothes, our skin, our memories.

We cared for the detainees in every aspect. We emptied their five-gallon buckets. We kept them calm, shuttled them to and from interrogation tents. As combat operations intensified, we began inprocessing more and more prisoners, men captured in firefights, dragged out of caves, or turned in by local warlords. It was relentless.

It was surreal. A few weeks prior, I'd been holding my newborn daughter. Now I was guarding prisoners captured in the caves of Tora Bora.

We worked long shifts in the heat and cold, surviving on MREs and instant coffee.

Nights were filled with the dull thump of mortars and the buzz of generators. Our job was to keep the perimeter tight, ensure humane treatment, and remain vigilant.

I had just started to find rhythm in the chaos when everything changed.

I didn't deploy with the rest of my company for Operation Anaconda. On the eve of the mission, I was pulled aside.

Karen had called the unit's Rear Detachment First Sergeant and told them she no longer wanted to be a mother. She was abandoning the kids.

The Red Cross followed up with an official message: Karen had suffered a severe mental breakdown. She'd left Jakub and newborn Zoe home alone.

The kids were safe. But everything else was in chaos.

It didn't feel real.

I was standing in one of the harshest places on Earth, preparing to fight terrorists, and suddenly I was on a flight home. Head spinning. Heart racing. Mind trapped between two wars.

When I landed stateside, the Rear Detachment First Sergeant met me at the airport. He drove me home.

We talked during the 45-minute ride about duty, about sacrifice, about what had to be done. There was no time for emotion. I needed to take care of the kids.

I walked into the house.

Bottles were everywhere.

Diapers unbagged. Food is rotting in the sink. Jakub, three years old, tried to be strong but clung to me like a shadow. Zoe was too little to understand anything but the comfort of my arms.

In that moment, I realized something no school or training had prepared me for: Combat is not always the greatest test of a leader. Sometimes it's coming home.

The Soldier in me took over. I stabilized the situation. I did inventory. I made phone calls. I packed the kids' bags with trembling hands. I called my parents and told them I was coming.

I loaded the car with quiet fury and drove through the night to Indiana.

My parents didn't ask a lot of questions. They just opened the door.

I remember the moment I handed Zoe to my mother. Her tiny body sagged with exhaustion, but her eyes locked on mine, like she knew I wasn't staying.

Jakub cried when I hugged him goodbye. He didn't want me to go. He'd already been abandoned once.

I made promises. I told him I'd be back.

Then I got in the car and drove away.

I wept halfway back to Ft. Bragg.

When I returned to Kandahar, it was like time had folded.

Same dust.

Same noise.

Same war.

But I was different.

Something had cracked in me. I was now a single father in a combat zone. Every IED, every gunshot, every mission, wasn't just about survival anymore. It was about getting home.

There was a steeliness that took hold of me.

I didn't talk much anymore. I volunteered for everything. I stayed busy so my mind wouldn't wander.

But sometimes, in the still moments between patrols, I'd find myself staring at the horizon, wondering if Zoe remembered me. Wondering if Jakub would grow up angry. Wondering if Karen would ever recover.

I stopped being afraid to die. And started being afraid to fail.

Mail was slow. I barely heard from home. When I did, it was a short letter from my mom saying the kids were okay. That was all I needed.

That one sentence kept me moving.

I started carrying pictures in my pocket, Jakub in his Halloween costume, Zoe wrapped in a pink blanket. I showed them to no one. But when the nights stretched too long, and the missions went too dark, I'd pull them out like armor.

One mission, we were ambushed near a wadi outside Kandahar. The air turned to static. We returned fire. Called in support. Fought like hell. I took cover behind my vehicle, heart pounding, bullets cracking past my head.

I thought of Zoe.

Of Jakub. Not of death, but of failure.

Of not coming home.

That fear turned to focus turned to fury. And we survived. I didn't just want to win. I needed to survive. I needed to live long enough to raise them. There were other missions. Other days that blurred into a haze of dust and gunpowder.

But what I remember most is the quiet.

The silence between explosions.

The stillness after a mission. The hollow moments when I would sit alone, weapon across my lap, and feel the ache of absence.

My body was in the fight. My soul was home.

When the tour ended, I brought my kids back to Ft Bragg and started a new life. Karen was gone for good. No forwarding address. Just a trail of court dates and medical records.

I filed for divorce. I got custody. I stayed in the Army.

I hung up my boots at night only to lace them up again the next morning, because I had two kids depending on me, and I wasn't going to fail them.

Leadership doesn't always come with a rank. Sometimes it comes with a car seat in the back of a dusty sedan, two tired kids in tow, and the quiet resolve to rebuild from ashes.

It wasn't heroic. It wasn't glamorous. But it was necessary.

I was 27 years old and starting over.

I cooked. I cleaned. I read bedtime stories. I patched scraped knees and taught Jakub how to tie his shoes. I warmed bottles and whispered lullabies to Zoe when she couldn't sleep.

There were moments I felt like I was drowning. When the bills piled up. When the loneliness pressed down like a weight.

But I never let the kids see it. I smiled when I wanted to scream. I laughed when I wanted to cry.

That's what leaders do.

One night, Jakub asked me if I was going back to war.

I knelt down, looked him in the eye, and said,
"No. Not for a long time. Right now, my mission is you."

He nodded and climbed into bed.

That night, I sat on the couch and realized something: I was exactly where I was supposed to be.

Not on a battlefield. Not in a Humvee. But right there, in a quiet house with two sleeping children.

And I made a decision:

I would rebuild. I would be more than what I had lost. I would **lead anyway.**

Leadership Debrief: The Mission at Home

- War doesn't always come with a uniform. **Sometimes it comes with silence, tears, and uncertainty.**
- The mission doesn't end when you come home, it just changes shape.
- Leadership is stepping up when no one else will, even when it costs you your dreams.
- Courage isn't just kicking in doors. **It's facing the chaos of family and rebuilding from nothing.**
- Your ***why*** becomes your fuel. **For me, it was two kids who didn't get a choice.**
- Don't confuse quiet strength with weakness. **Some of the strongest battles are never seen.**

SPC Long is taking a break for some tea with an Afghan local in a rose garden in the desert. June 2002.

Chapter 11
The Weight Between Wars

It was during this time that I met Alice.

She was a fellow Reservist\, kind, patient, and warm in ways I hadn't realized I was missing. We first crossed paths during a routine administrative weekend. I was reviewing files when she came into the room needing assistance with her personnel records. She had a calm energy, the kind that steadied the air around her. We made small talk, then talked some more. I wasn't looking for anything, but maybe that's why it worked.

Alice didn't judge me for the baggage I carried. She didn't flinch when I told her about Karen or the kids. Instead, she asked how *they* were. What they liked. How *was I* really doing? Her questions weren't laced with pity. They were laced with care.

We started talking more regularly. We went on walks with the kids. We shared meals and stories. She made Jakub laugh. She held Zoe like she was her own. And slowly, something began to shift in me.

I started to feel like a man again, not just a father. Not just a Soldier. But someone worthy of love and partnership. Alice reminded me that I didn't have to be perfect to be present. That leadership at home didn't mean stoicism; it meant vulnerability.

We weren't without our challenges. I was guarded. She was patient. I struggled to trust. She gave me space. And in that space, I grew.

She didn't try to replace Karen.
She simply stood beside me as I rebuilt.

The kids adored her.
Jakub started calling her his "buddy."
Zoe would reach for her arms.
I hadn't expected it, but I was grateful for it.
The three of us had been surviving.
With Alice, we began living.

I remember one specific Saturday morning. The kids had crawled into bed with us, Zoe giggling as Jakub pretended to be a tickle monster. I lay there watching them, overwhelmed by something I hadn't felt in a long time, peace. That quiet moment, those sleepy smiles, they meant more than any medal ever could.

In January 2003, Alice moved into the apartment I was renting in Fayetteville. Things were transitioning well. She got a job as a hospice aide. The kids grew even closer to her.

I could see how much they loved her in the way Jakub ran to greet her after work, and how Zoe curled up on her lap without hesitation. She brought her mother down from Michigan to meet us, a quiet gesture that meant everything. It felt like the beginning of a family built not on convenience or obligation, but on choice.

One night, after the kids were asleep, Alice sat with me on the couch and shared her own struggles growing up, how her strength was forged through hardship. She told me that being here, with the kids and me, felt like redemption for her, too. I realized then that healing wasn't something you did alone. It was something you did in the company of someone who chose to stay.

Life between the wars was never simple. But it was sacred.

It was the stretch of time that reminded me what I was fighting for, Not just survival, but connection, healing, and home.

The world beyond our apartment walls was growing increasingly volatile. President George W. Bush had begun making public statements about the imminent threat posed by Saddam Hussein, warning of weapons of mass destruction and drawing connections to global terrorism.

I watched the speeches and press briefings with a mix of disbelief and frustration. It all felt manufactured, like a vendetta wrapped in patriotism. To me, this wasn't about national security. It was about settling an old score, revenge for the attempted assassination of Bush's father during a visit to Kuwait a decade earlier.

The administration worked hard to link Saddam to the terror networks responsible for 9/11, but the evidence felt flimsy.

Still, the war drums were beating louder by the day.

Then the phone rang. April 4th, 2003, the call I wasn't ready for.

Orders had come down. We were deploying to Kuwait in preparation for the war in Iraq.

My stomach dropped as the weight of it sank in. I stared at the phone for a few seconds after hanging up, knowing life was about to shift again.

When I told Alice, she didn't panic. She didn't cry or beg me to stay.

She simply nodded, took a deep breath, and said,

"We'll be okay. I'll take care of the kids. You do what you need to do."

Her eyes said everything her voice didn't. There was fear. But also strength.

I don't know where this angel came from, but I was damn sure glad she showed up when she did.

That evening, I packed my ruck with practiced hands, but my heart wasn't in it.

I glanced at Jakub's drawing taped to the fridge. Zoe's pacifier is on the coffee table. Alice's shoes are by the door.

I was leaving behind my world and everything that grounded me, To step back into uncertainty.

As I closed the apartment door, I felt a lump in my throat that I couldn't swallow.

I drove away with a storm in my chest, Equal parts duty and dread.

This time, I wasn't just a Soldier heading into combat. I was a father and a partner, leaving behind the most fragile and beautiful part of my life. And that made the sacrifice feel even heavier.

Leadership Debrief: Between the Wars

- Healing isn't linear. It comes in waves; some days you thrive, some days you survive.
- Leadership at home requires the same intentionality as
- leadership in uniform.
- Vulnerability isn't weakness. It's how trust is built, and love is formed.
- Presence is power. Sometimes just showing up, consistently and honestly, is the bravest thing you can do.
- Love, when it's real, doesn't fix you. It reminds you that you're worth rebuilding.
- The quiet seasons between battles matter. They shape the kind of leader, partner, and parent you become.

SPC Preston and SGT Long are waiting at Green Ramp for a transport to Kuwait. April 4, 2003.

Chapter 12
The Streets of Mosul

Deployment to Kuwait in April 2003 felt like a rewind and a reset, a loop I had barely escaped, now sucking me back in. But this time, the stakes were higher. I wasn't just a Soldier deploying. I was a father, leaving behind two small children and a woman I had trusted with our fragile new life.

The flight into Kuwait was thick with silence and jet fuel. The moment we stepped off the aircraft, the heat hit us like a wall. Unlike Afghanistan, where we built our existence from dust, Kuwait was purgatory. Everything was temporary. Everything was waiting.

We trained. Cleaned gear. Ran missions in the sand. But mostly, we waited. Every day was a countdown to uncertainty. Every night, I called home when I could. We spoke in fragments, her voice braver than the emotions hiding behind it. Neither of us asked the hard questions: *What if I didn't come back? What if she couldn't hold it together?*

Then, in May, we got the order: roll north.

Convoying into Iraq felt like stepping into the unknown without a map. We moved in long, slow trails of armored vehicles across the desert. Every overpass was a threat. Every village is a question mark. When we finally reached Mosul, it was chaos wrapped in the shell of a city. The regime had collapsed, but what remained was raw, angry, and unpredictable.

Our daily mission became a rotating gauntlet: Patrols. Humanitarian drops. Building security. Raids. One day, we were peacekeepers; the next, warriors.

And then came July 22, 2003.

That day, we were briefed on a high-value target mission. Uday and Qusay Hussein, Saddam's sons, were believed to be hiding in a compound in Mosul.

The atmosphere shifted instantly. We knew this was big.

I wasn't on the breach team, but my squad set outer security. The irefight started like thunder, sudden, violent, echoing through the alleys. For hours, it raged. Anti-tank missiles slammed into the structure, ripping it apart piece by piece. We watched as the regime's future burned in front of us.

When it was over, their bodies were pulled from the rubble. It was supposed to feel like a victory. But it didn't. Not really. It just felt like the beginning of something darker.

Not long after came the mission that haunts me most.

Late one night, we responded to a distress call. A sister platoon was under attack, pinned down by sustained enemy fire. We loaded into our Humvee and pushed out fast.

The sky was clear. Too clear.

When our vehicle hit a patch of loose gravel and slid into a ditch, we were stuck, completely exposed. And then the firefight lit up the night.

Tracers carved through the air like blood-red lightning, drawing fiery arcs across the black sky. It looked like a Fourth of July show from hell.

We could hear the firefight intensifying, rapid bursts, shouted commands, explosions in the distance. We didn't wait. I gave the order.

We dismounted and began the two-mile movement on foot. Every step was calculated. Every corner is a potential ambush. We moved fast, bounding and covering, hearts racing.

My mind was clear. My purpose was fixed.

When we arrived, we reinforced the perimeter, supported our brothers, and helped push back the attackers. That night earned me an Army Commendation Medal.

But the medal means nothing. What mattered was that none of my men died.

In August 2003, I was reassigned to a Long Range Surveillance Company in Zakho, near the Turkish border. The mission was unlike any I'd had: Recruit and train the first Iraqi Border Patrol.

We worked with Kurdish Peshmerga, fierce, loyal fighters hardened by decades of survival. We trained over 150 men in anti-smuggling operations, tactical patrolling, prisoner handling, and counterterrorism tactics.

We built a training program from the ground up. We built trust. We built capability.

And for the first time in months, I felt like I was part of something constructive.

Back home, Alice was holding it all together, or so I thought.

She cared for Jakub and Zoe, held down a job, managed the household, and sent letters that painted a picture of stability. She never let on that things were breaking. She never said *she* was breaking.

In October 2003, I returned to Mosul. Zakho had changed me. The war had matured into something more complex than enemies and allies.

It was about people, power, and persistence.

I came back to my unit more focused than ever, ready to finish the mission.

I had been thinking about home more than usual.
Maybe it was the return to familiar rhythms.
Maybe it was the strain of trying to do so much with so little.

I missed my kids.
I missed the feeling that everything I was doing *mattered* to the people I loved.

I began to imagine the day I'd finally walk through the front door and be welcomed like a hero.

Then, one evening, I called home.

Her voice cracked the moment she answered.

"We need to talk."

Silence. And then,

"I can't do this anymore."

She told me she was 22. Too young to be raising two kids. She told me she had been seeing someone else—a man from the apartment complex. She told me she needed more than what I could give from across the ocean.

I felt the floor fall out from under me. Rage. Sadness. Disbelief. All of it came crashing in like a wave I wasn't ready for.

After everything,

After all the promises...

After all, I was fighting for...

It was happening again.

That night, I didn't sleep. I lay awake on my cot, staring at the plywood ceiling of our makeshift barracks, wondering how everything I had built had crumbled again.

The desert felt colder that night.

The stars above, so distant and silent, seemed to mock the storm tearing through my chest.

I thought about my kids…Jakub's laughter, Zoe's little hand in mine.

I thought about the sacrifices I had made. The blood I watched soak into the soil.

All for what?

To be left behind again.

To be betrayed, again.

I had walked into firefights without blinking. But this? This gutted me.

And still, I woke up the next morning. I geared up.

I went back to work.

Because that's what Soldiers do.

Leadership Debrief: The Second War

- True leadership often requires sacrifice without recognition.
- When everything feels out of control, control what you can: your discipline, your decisions, your integrity.
- Courage isn't the absence of fear. It's acting in spite of it.
- People at home carry a weight just as heavy as the one we shoulder in combat.
- Building something, whether a patrol or a family, takes time, presence, and belief.
- Every war changes you. But coming home means deciding who you want to be **next**.

SGT Long on patrol with a Kurdish Peshmerga Soldier after completing Iraqi Border Patrol training on the Turkish border.

Chapter 13
Ashes and Aftermath

Coming home from Iraq in late 2003 felt like returning to a house fire that had already burned to the ground. I was exhausted, emotionally splintered, and unsure what life I was coming back to.
The mission was over, but the war inside me had just begun.

I had imagined the reunion a hundred different ways, visions of hugs, shared meals, and laughter with Alice and the kids. I thought maybe, just maybe, the sacrifice had been worth it if it meant coming back to something whole.

Instead, the closer I got to the apartment, the more pressure I felt in my chest. It wasn't jet lag. It was dread. Something deep inside me already knew.

When I arrived back in Fayetteville, it wasn't relief I felt.
It was confirmation.

I unlocked the door, expecting tension, maybe quiet guilt.
But I found Alice in the bedroom, getting ready for a date.
With *him.*
The man from downstairs.

Her hair was done. Makeup perfect.
A dress I didn't recognize clung to her like an insult.

"I thought you were going to Indiana," she said casually,
as if I'd just returned from the grocery store.

"I wanted to talk," I said, my voice low and strained.
"This can't be how we end it."

But it already had.

She didn't flinch.
Didn't stumble.
Just kept getting ready.

My parents had driven down from Indiana to pick up Jakub and Zoe, knowing I would need time, space, to figure out what came next. They had taken the kids north, shielding them from the emotional wreckage now smoldering inside these walls.

I stood there, watching her slide earrings into her ears, like I wasn't even real. Like the war, the letters, the promises, we never happened.

I was a ghost in my own home. Everything I had endured, the gunfire, the fear, the heat, the sleepless nights, the sickening phone call from Mosul, had brought me back to this.

Alone.
Unwanted.
Discarded.
Again.

After she left for her date, I didn't know what to do. The apartment was too small to contain my rage. Too quiet to hold my grief.

I grabbed my keys and walked. I walked nearly ten miles, through unfamiliar neighborhoods, past gas stations, strip malls, and quiet, dark stretches of road.

My boots hit the pavement like they were marching through a battlefield. My thoughts spun, numb. My heart raced, but I felt hollow.

I replayed everything, her voice on the phone in Iraq, the silence that followed, the moment I opened that door.

What had I missed? What could I have done differently?

Each mile peeled away another layer of denial.

I had fought wars on two continents, but this betrayal cut deeper than any bullet.

The silence around me screamed louder than explosions ever could.

Hours later, my phone rang.

It was her. Her voice was shaking. I could hear the panic.

"Where are you?" she asked. "I didn't know if something happened to you."

"I just needed to walk," I said. My voice was flat. Not angry. Not accusatory. Just empty. She found me walking along a side street a few miles from the apartment.

She pulled up slowly. Headlights dimmed. I got in.

We didn't speak right away.

Eventually, the silence cracked. We talked.

Not accusations. Not screaming. Just raw, aching conversation between two people who knew they couldn't undo what had been done.

There were no winners here. No villains. No saints. Just two broken souls trying to explain the unexplainable.

She cried. I listened. I asked why.

She didn't have all the answers. I didn't either.

There was no healing in that car, only honesty.

A moment stripped of pretense.

We talked about loneliness. Resentment. Needs unmet. About distance, not just physical, but emotional.

We admitted what we'd been afraid to say out loud: Maybe we were never built to last. Maybe we both wanted to believe a lie because it felt better than the truth. That night, I slept alone in a place that no longer felt like mine.

I lay on the bed we once shared, staring at the ceiling while the weight of everything pressed down on my chest.

The walls were silent, but judgmental. My fists clenched in the dark. My thoughts circled like vultures.

The next morning, I packed.

My hands moved like a machine. I didn't know what I was packing for, a fresh start or just an escape.

My parents were already in Indiana with Jakub and Zoe. They knew what I needed before I did.

Driving north felt like peeling off scabs that hadn't finished healing. The highway stretched out, gray and indifferent.

My thoughts swung wildly between anger and gratitude.

Anger at Alice, for giving up, for giving in, for moving on while I was still in uniform.

But also, gratitude, for clarity. For the chance to rebuild without illusion. When I picked up the kids, Jakub ran to me. Zoe was quieter.

She held me, but cautiously, like I was a stranger.

And that's when it hit me:

She didn't recognize me. Not really.

I had missed so much. Been gone too long.

To her, I wasn't Daddy. I was a uniformed ghost trying to reclaim a role I'd abandoned.

That broke me in a way, combat never could.

But when she finally leaned into me, something cracked open.

Not just in her, in *me*, too.

Driving back to Ft Bragg with Jakub and Zoe, I knew I had to leave the Army.

No one else was going to raise my kids. That burden was mine now.

And I accepted it, with a heavy heart and clear eyes.

In that moment, I realized something profound:

This was the only war that mattered now**.** Keeping them safe. Raising them right. Becoming the kind of man they'd be proud to call Dad.

Everything was broken. But I still had them.

I still had Jakub and Zoe.

It was time to rebuild, again. Not as a Soldier. Not as a husband. But as a father.

Leadership Debrief: Ashes and Aftermath

- Betrayal can hit harder than bullets. Healing from it takes longer.
- When someone shows you they've moved on, believe them, and move on stronger.
- Children deserve a version of you that isn't consumed by someone else's decision.
- Trust, once shattered, requires boundaries, not just forgiveness.
- Coming home is never simple. You must redefine what "home" even means.
- **Lead anyway**, even when the mission changes.

Chapter 14
The Final Salute

Driving back to Fort Bragg with Jakub and Zoe in the backseat, the decision was already made. I had wrestled with it for weeks, but now, watching my son fall asleep against the window and my daughter chewing quietly on a fruit snack, it was crystal clear: I had to get out of the Army. No one else was going to raise these kids. That job was mine now. Solely. Wholly. Irrevocably mine.

The guilt was overwhelming. I knew what this meant for the Soldiers I had served alongside. I knew what it meant for the unit. Walking away felt like betrayal, even if it was the only move left to play. But when I weighed my oath to the Army against my responsibility to these two small humans, the choice wasn't really a choice at all.

Back at Bragg, I started the paperwork for a hardship discharge. Some leaders understood. Others didn't.

One senior NCO I'd served with for years looked me in the eye and said, "So you're just walking away?"

I didn't answer. What could I say that would make sense to someone who hadn't come home to find his life in tatters and his kids nearly strangers?

Alice and I, against all odds, began to reconnect. The pain was still fresh, the wounds still raw, but there was something deeper beneath the wreckage, something worth exploring again.

We didn't rush.
We didn't pretend it hadn't happened.
But we talked. *Really* talked.
Not just about the kids or schedules, but about *us*.
Who we were.
What we wanted.
And how we might find a better way forward.

Slowly, we found our way back to each other, not as the people we were, but as the people we were becoming.

I wasn't a Soldier anymore. She wasn't just the woman who broke my heart. We were survivors of our own mess, trying to stitch together a new beginning.

She said she wanted to move back to Michigan, closer to her family. She needed support. And honestly, so did I. The idea of starting over in a familiar place, with fewer ghosts and more helping hands, made sense, so I agreed.

When my discharge orders came through, it felt surreal. One chapter of my life closed not with a bang, but a quiet sigh.

I packed our belongings, loaded up the car again, and said goodbye to the post that had shaped so much of my adult life.

I took a deep breath, glanced at my kids in the rearview mirror, and turned the wheel toward Michigan.

The drive north was long and reflective. Each mile put more distance between the man I had been and the one I was becoming.

We stopped at rest areas and gas stations, sang silly songs, ate snacks, and made new memories.

I still didn't know what life would look like.
But I knew who I was doing it for.

Alice's family welcomed us. It was awkward at first. But they could see the effort. We didn't get our own place right away; we moved in with her dad, who offered us a roof and a little breathing room while we got back on our feet.

It wasn't ideal. But it was safe. And it gave the kids a sense of stability we hadn't felt in months.

Her dad was kind but quiet. And while the space was tight, the gesture meant everything.

Soon after, we found a modest house back in Northern Indiana, unpacked slowly, and began to build a routine.

Jakub started second grade. Zoe learned new words.

Eventually, I got my job back at the juvenile detention center. It wasn't glorious, but it was solid.

At night, I'd sit outside in the cold Indiana air, a hoodie pulled tight, coffee in hand, thinking about the path behind me and the uncertain road ahead.

But for once, it didn't feel like failure.

It felt like faith.

Faith that I could be the father they needed.

Faith that redemption wasn't a place you reached, but a road you walked, one step at a time. And Alice stayed. She kept showing up.

We rebuilt something quite and sturdy. It wasn't perfect. But it was real.

We laughed again. We fought sometimes. But we kept choosing each other, and the kids. That meant more than words ever could.

Abigail was born in 2005, a new beginning wrapped in pink blankets and midnight feedings.

Her arrival felt like a second chance at fatherhood, not as a Soldier torn between duty and home, but as a man fully present.

That same year, Alice and I got married.

It wasn't extravagant, just a quiet ceremony in her mother's living room in Michigan.

No fancy venue.
No big audience.

Just close family, soft promises, and the quiet determination to keep building something real.

It wasn't the kind of wedding you see in movies.
But it was honest. And for us, that honesty mattered more than anything else.

I had left a battlefield behind. But I hadn't stopped serving. I was just fighting a different kind of war, the war to build a life worth living, to become a man my kids could look up to.

And I was winning.

Leadership Debrief: The Final Salute

- Sometimes, the bravest thing you can do is walk away from the life you built to protect the people who need you most.
- Leadership means showing up where you're most needed, even if it costs you everything else.
- Forgiveness isn't always about rebuilding; it's sometimes about repurposing.
- The end of one uniform doesn't mean the end of service.
- You can start over. Not with a bang, but with a thousand quiet choices to keep going.
- **Lead anyway**, even when the battlefield is your own living room.

Chapter 15
The New Badge

Leaving the Army didn't mean I stopped serving. It just meant the uniform changed.

I needed a new identity, something to tether me to the world again, something that could give structure to the chaos of starting over.

The war might've ended for me, but the battle to rebuild a life was just beginning.

So I put in an application to a sheriff's department in Northern Indiana. They were hiring patrol officers. I figured my background might get me in the door. I didn't expect it to become another defining chapter of my life.

Then came the call: Interview. Physical agility test. Polygraph. Background check.

And then one day, a brown envelope in the mailbox: I was in.

The police academy started in the spring of 2006. I was 30 years old, one of the oldest recruits in Class 165.

I wasn't just older. I was experienced. Hardened. I had seen things my classmates only knew from training simulations or TV.

In the final weeks of the academy, they elected me class president. Not because I asked to be.

But because leadership recognizes leadership.

I ran morning PT. Helped cadets study for tests.
Talked people off the ledge when they were ready to quit.

We graduated a month later. I gave the class speech.

It felt like stepping into something solid again. Purpose. Community. Order.

Back on the street, I was assigned a field training officer. The rhythms of patrol were different from combat, but some instincts transferred cleanly:

Scan the windows. Watch the hands. Read the room. Know when to talk. Know when to shut up.

I wanted SWAT. Bad. My military experience made me a strong candidate.

But law enforcement is political. There's always someone watching, waiting for you to either screw up or impress.

I didn't have time to wait. So I went all in.

That's when the call came in.

Domestic violence. A neighbor heard screaming next door.

I was only a couple of streets over. I blacked out my lights and approached silently, parking a house away to stay unseen.

This wasn't my first domestic. But something felt… off.

A twisting in my gut I couldn't shake. I crept toward the large picture windows.

Inside, I saw a large man, shirtless, covered in blood, pacing into the kitchen.

The screams were coming from a back bedroom.

I radioed for backup. Told them to step it up.

I paused.

Every part of my training told me to wait. Backup was en route. Policy said wait. Safety said Wait.

But instinct? Instinct said go**.**

I entered the house.

He didn't see me. I followed him quietly down the hallway.

He opened the bedroom door.

I drew my Taser.

"Police! Let me see your hands!"

He turned with a knife.

"Drop the knife!" I shouted.

He froze. I didn't. I deployed the Taser. He dropped, but one of the wires came loose.

I didn't wait.

Drive stun. Again. I cuffed him, alone, relieved, furious.

Still no backup.

Turns out the rookie who was supposed to assist me got lost. This was before GPS in every car.

I cleared the rest of the house.

In the bedroom, a girl, no older than 12, stood frozen.
Eyes wide. Shocked.

Behind her, the bathroom door was splintered, blood smeared across it where the man had tried to stab through.

His wife was inside. Shaking. Alive.

She looked at me and whispered,

"Thank you."

Later, we learned he'd gone for a second knife. I had walked in just in time.

The next day, the Sergeant called me into his office. He reprimanded me.

For *not* shooting the man.

He cited the "21-foot rule", a guideline about how close a knife-wielding attacker can be before lethal force is justified.

He said I violated policy. Said I was reckless. Said this would likely disqualify me from SWAT.

I looked him in the eye and said,

"You weren't there. That man was five feet from his daughter. I acted when I saw the knife. I ended the threat without killing him, without adding more trauma to a girl who's already seen too much."

He didn't care. To him, I was too soft. To me, I had done the job right.

I was furious. But more determined than ever.

Three months later, I got the invite to SWAT tryouts.

It was brutal, a three-day gauntlet of physical, mental, and tactical testing.

I didn't just pass. I crushed it.

After the final marksmanship test, which I thought I'd done average on, the team leader approached me.

His name was Mike.

"You're on the team," he said. **"Marksman. Scout."**

"Why sniper?" I asked.

He looked me dead in the eye.

"Because I know that if it ever comes down to it, you won't hesitate."

I nodded slowly. I wasn't a killer. I was a protector.

But he was right.

If the moment came again, if someone's life was on the line, I wouldn't freeze.

And that's when I realized the difference between my leadership now and the man I used to be:

It wasn't about being the loudest voice in the room. Or the toughest. Or the most feared.

It was about knowing who you are when it counts.

Leadership Debrief: The New Badge

- You can find a new purpose after pain, but you have to be willing to rebuild.
- Leadership doesn't require a title; people follow those who step up when others freeze.
- Sometimes the right decision isn't the easiest or most popular one.
- Courage isn't just facing danger; it's choosing restraint when violence tempts you.
- Recognition doesn't define you. Integrity does.
- **Lead anyway**, even when your reputation walks into the room before you do.

Deputy Long shooting at the 2008 Area SWAT Challenge. This was a hostage situation at 200 yards. He went on to win the challenge.

Chapter 16
Rising and Cracking

By 2008, I was at the height of my law enforcement career, at least, on paper. I had built a name as one of the most aggressive and effective warrant officers in the county, especially in the fight against meth. I hunted meth cooks like they were on my personal hit list, because in many ways, they were. Every lab we shut down, every dealer we cuffed, was one less family destroyed by that poison.

I was relentless. Precise. And I loved the work.

That year, I was named Officer of the Year. I had stepped into a field training officer role, mentoring younger deputies, teaching tactics, presence, and how to command a scene. When a warrant needed to be served and things could go sideways, they called me. I didn't flinch. I didn't hesitate. And everyone knew it.

But while I was thriving professionally, my personal life was collapsing.

At home, my marriage to Alice was unraveling. The trust was long gone. Her affairs weren't rumors; they were reality. I buried myself in overtime, in operations, in anything that kept me out of the house. I told myself it was noble, that I was providing, serving, protecting. But the truth was simpler:

I didn't want to be home.

I couldn't fix what was broken, so I ran.

Money was tight. Communication was dead. And beneath the tactical armor, I was unraveling.

I could command a breach. But I couldn't command peace in my own house.

The Raid

It was a bitter winter night. We got a call, meth warrant, north side. Another known dealer. Another dirty house. Another chance to make a dent.

I was running point again. Standard. I was the tip of the spear. When lives were on the line, they wanted someone who wouldn't freeze.

The captain that night was a Navy vet turned ranking officer. Sharp? Sure. But deeply insecure. He wore his rank like a costume, constantly reminding everyone who was in charge. That's not leadership. That's fear wearing brass.

Despite intel confirming the front door as the active entry point, he insisted on a rear breach. Chain of command. We didn't argue.

We loaded up, rolled out, and stacked on the backside of the house.

Seven-man entry team. I was first. The captain was fourth. My MP5 was trained forward as the breacher readied his stance.

The radio crackled:

"Execute."

Thud.
Nothing.
Again, Thud.
Still nothing.

The battering ram hit the door five times. It wouldn't give.
Every second that passed was a gift to the suspects, time to flush the stash or arm themselves.

I hesitated for a half-breath.

I knew I should wait.
I knew the captain had to call it.
I knew protocol.

But lives don't wait for protocol.

"Failed breach, failed breach, move to the front of the house!" I shouted.

Dead air. Then, finally, grudgingly:

"Failed breach. Move front."

We regrouped. The front door gave on the first hit. Flashbang in, BOOM. I pushed through smoke and chaos. A man bolted down the hallway.

"Police! Search warrant! Get on the ground!"

He didn't listen.

He made a break for the bathroom. I chased him, shouting commands. He reached the toilet, ready to dump the stash.

I drove my MP5 into his back like a sledgehammer. He collapsed forward, knocking the tank off the base. I zip-tied him to the floor.

Drugs secured. Suspect down. No shots fired.

We cleared the rest of the house. Turns out the rear door had a tanning bed braced against it. A five-second walkthrough by the undercover earlier would've caught that.

But the intel failed.
We did what we had to do.

At debrief, I said it straight:
"Intel was garbage. We should've shifted faster."

The captain snapped.
"I'm the scene commander. You don't call failed breaches."

I didn't argue.
I just stared.

Then the same sergeant who once tried to write me up for not shooting a man in front of his daughter chimed in:

"Long was unprofessional. He cursed at the suspect."

Yeah. I did.

And I got compliance without a drop of blood. Sometimes, you don't use polite language; you use effective language.

No one backed me. Just a few head nods.

Another successful mission. Another silent victory.

Another chip carved into a career I was beginning to resent.

The Breaking Point

Tension was constant. Every shift pulled on a fraying rope.

Then something strange happened.

The same captain who had questioned my decisions…asked me to write the SWAT team's Standard Operating Procedures.

"We need something tight. Professional."

I poured everything I had into it.

When I handed it in, he issued me a formal letter of commendation. Called it the most complete SOP he'd ever seen.

But that didn't fix the cracks. I was still angry. Still out of place.
I missed the structure. The clarity. The mission.

A buddy of mine, a fellow vet, noticed.

"Why don't you come back in? National Guard's always looking for MPs."

I laughed it off. But the thought lingered.

On May 30, 2007, I raised my right hand and swore in again. This time as a Sergeant in the Indiana Army National Guard.

The next day, I handed my orders to my sergeant at the department. No congratulations. Just a write-up.

For taking a second job without permission.

Didn't matter.

Because when I put that uniform back on, something inside me clicked.

I remembered who I was.

Not just a cop.

Not just a soldier.

A leader.

A protector.

A man with a mission.

What I Learned

- Doing the right thing doesn't always earn applause. Sometimes, it earns a reprimand.
- Rank doesn't equal respect. Some leaders earn it. Others demand it because they lack it.
- In chaos, your instinct becomes your identity. Train it well.
- Anger, when unchecked, becomes poison. It clouds even your clearest judgment.
- Protocol matters, but principle matters more. When lives are on the line, action beats bureaucracy.
- You don't need to be liked to lead. You need to be ready.

Leadership Debrief: Lessons from the Breach

- Experience is a weapon, but only if wielded with humility.
- The loudest person in the room isn't the leader. Leadership shows up in **calm, decisive action** when the plan falls apart.
- Poor leadership punishes initiative. But real leaders act, even when it costs them.
- Anger left unchecked becomes your enemy. Leadership is learning to fight the battle without becoming the war.
- Adversity reveals character. When others deflect, defame, or dismiss you, **respond with execution**.
- Purpose is your compass in chaos. When everything breaks, **mission, meaning, and code of honor** keep you moving.

I didn't take the point on that raid to be a hero. I took the point because I knew what it meant to be responsible for the man next to me.

I didn't curse out of rage; I cursed to save lives.

Maybe I wasn't polished. But I was ready when the breach failed. Steady when others stalled. Present when it counted.

And when the politics got loud, I got louder through action.

I never needed to be liked. I needed to be ready.

And sometimes… that's what leadership really is.

Chapter 17
The Recruiter and the Reckoning

The Invitation

By 2009, I wasn't actively searching for a way out, but I was tired enough to walk through the next open door.

The Sheriff's Department had taken more out of me than I'd realized. SWAT raids. Department politics. Calls involving screaming children, overdosed teenagers, and blood-soaked kitchens.

It wasn't one moment that broke me. It was the accumulation. Trauma doesn't always come from a single blast. Sometimes it comes from the steady drip of darkness.

I was holding it together, technically. But I wasn't laughing. I wasn't sleeping.

I wasn't living. I was enduring.

One National Guard drill weekend, a recruiter pulled me aside after formation.

He'd heard about my background, combat deployments, law enforcement, SWAT, and something about it stuck.

"You'd make a great recruiter," he said.

I laughed.

"Aren't recruiters just the guys who lie to high school kids and dump them into bad jobs to hit quota?"

He didn't flinch. Just smiled.

"That's what people think," he said. **"But it doesn't have to be that way."**

I didn't buy it.

I had known a few recruiters, none of them exactly inspired trust. I figured it was all smoke and mirrors.

But he didn't press. He didn't make a pitch. He just stayed in touch, quietly.

A few texts. A random call. Nothing pushy. Just presence.

And then, when he heard I was struggling with the department, he said something that landed:

"This job could give you a new mission, one where people actually thank you."

I didn't say yes. But I started to think about it.

The more I thought, the more I realized what I had lost: purpose.

I had once led Soldiers in war zones. Mentored teammates through adversity.

Helped train the first Iraqi Border Patrol unit.

But lately, my job had become a slow-motion tragedy, a constant tour of other people's worst days.

I didn't want to just survive anymore. I wanted to serve, and I wanted it to matter. In June 2009, I accepted a full-time Active Guard Reserve (AGR) position with the Indiana Army National Guard. By law, the Sheriff's Department had to hold my job for up to five years. That gave me a buffer. A risk worth taking. I was stationed in Elkhart, not far from home.

It felt like a clean slate.

That illusion didn't last long.

The Pep Talk

On day one, they sent me to a statewide recruiter meeting in

Indianapolis. I didn't know a soul. Sat in the back. Watched.

Over a hundred recruiters filled the room, laughing, slapping backs like it was a reunion. Then the Sergeant Major walked in. Took the mic like he was about to deliver a pep talk.

Instead, he opened with:

"First, let's recognize the people holding the rest of us back."

He scanned the crowd.

"Elkhart recruiters, stand up."

I stood, unsure. Two others stood beside me. I figured maybe it was a joke. A team-building thing.

I was wrong.

"These guys," he declared, **"are the horse's ass of the battalion. Last place in every measurable category. Every single one."**

The room erupted in laughter.

I didn't laugh.

That was my welcome to the recruiting world. I sat down without a word.

But inside, something shifted.

I would never, ever, be called a horse's ass again.

The Ascent and the Unraveling

There was no onboarding. No handbook.
I was handed a government laptop, a set of car keys, a password to the Army recruiting system, and one simple directive:

Write two contracts a month, or else.

So I got to work.

My philosophy was simple: Be the recruiter I'd want my own kids to meet.

That meant no lies. No pressure. And no shoving a 17-year-old into a contract just to meet quota.

I sat with students and asked them about their dreams, not just their ASVAB scores. I helped with class schedules. Went to their games. Met their parents at the kitchen table.

I didn't push the Army. I translated it.

And something happened: people trusted me.

That first year, I wrote 34 contracts. Not just meeting the standard, obliterating it.

When the other two Elkhart recruiters left, I helped rebuild the team. Within a year, we went from the bottom of the battalion to the top in our region.

The same station that had been humiliated was now setting the pace.

I earned awards. Recognition. Invitations. People asked for my advice. I earned my Expert Recruiter Badge in just 18 months.

From the outside, it looked like everything was coming together.

But behind closed doors?

Everything was falling apart.

At home, Alice was back to her old patterns.
Late nights. Excuses.
I caught her, more than once, at another man's apartment.

The stories changed: study group, ride-along, friend in crisis.

I wanted to believe her. But I didn't.

And I was too emotionally drained to keep pretending.

Meanwhile, I was fighting my own war. Combat stress. Nightmares. Explosive anger. Anxiety so thick it felt like drowning in air.

Most nights, I stared at the ceiling in silence. Body still. Mind racing.

I was barely sleeping. I was angry, numb, and ashamed.

And too proud to ask for help.

The one person who saw through it was my recruiting partner, SFC James Van Huffel.

He had just returned from Iraq.

He knew the signs.

He didn't press. Just looked at me one day and said:

"There's a number you can call. Military OneSource. You don't have to suffer."

That night, I called.

I spilled everything.

The rage. The panic attacks. The hollowness I couldn't explain.

They connected me to a therapist and a military psychologist.

I was diagnosed with PTSD, major depressive disorder, and insomnia.

They gave me meds. I tried therapy.

But it often felt like I was picking at old wounds just to bleed again.

I cycled through providers, searching for one who understood both combat and law enforcement.

I never found them.

So I smiled at work.

And I drowned at home.

The Line I Wouldn't Cross

In late 2011, I was called into the Sergeant Major's office. The tone was off from the start.

Van Huffel, my partner, my friend, was under investigation. They accused him of falsifying enlistment documents.

I knew the man. He was many things. But dishonesty wasn't one of them.

They asked me to sign a sworn statement backing their claims.

I hadn't seen anything. And I wasn't about to lie.

Not about him. Not after he'd been the one person who saw me unravel and didn't flinch.

I said no. The Sergeant Major didn't like that.

He threatened to transfer me, over an hour away. Said my career would stall. That if I didn't "play ball," there'd be consequences.

I told him I had a backup plan: the Sheriff's Department.

His bluff didn't scare me.

I walked out of that office and submitted my resignation.

What Changed, and What Didn't

In 2012, I returned to the Sheriff's Department. Same building. Same cruiser. Same uniform. But I wasn't the same man.

I had stood my ground. Refused to compromise. I chose loyalty over convenience. Integrity over advancement.

Alice hadn't changed. But I had. And I wasn't going back. Some endings aren't dramatic. They're just overdue.

Leadership Debrief: Lessons from the Recruiting Years

- **Integrity outranks position.** I could've saved my job. I chose to save my soul.
- **Recruiting isn't about contracts.** It's about building futures, one conversation at a time.
- **People are the mission.** Whether it's a struggling teen or an NCO on the brink, don't forget who you're really serving.
- **You can be winning in public and still losing in private.** Awards don't fix trauma. Plaques don't cure pain.
- **When your values are on the line, stand firm.** If the system asks you to betray what you know is right, it's time to walk.

I didn't quit recruiting because I failed. I quit because they asked me to become someone I'm not.

I've seen betrayal in war, in marriage, in leadership. And I refused to become it.

Not for a ribbon.
Not for a title.
Not for a safer route.

Because loyalty is a leadership trait too. And if you don't stand for something, you'll fall for anything. So I stood. I walked. And I never looked back.

SSG Long during his first year as a recruiter with the Indiana Army National Guard.

Chapter 18
The Breaking Point

Coming back to the Sheriff's Department felt like slipping into an old uniform that no longer fit. Everything was where I'd left it, the same department, same patrol area, same role on the SWAT team. The same cliques. The same politics. The same low ceilings.

But I wasn't the same man who had walked away years earlier.

I'd seen war. Led men in combat. Recruited young people into a purpose. Clawed my way out of trauma. The department hadn't changed. But I had.

And that made every hallway feel a little more suffocating.

Still, I was trying to make it work. Again.

I encouraged Alice to apply for a position with the township fire department. She got it. For a brief moment, I believed we were turning a corner. We were both employed. Our finances weren't perfect, but they were stable. Between us, we had four kids now, Jakub, Zoe, Abigail, and our youngest, Madeline, born in 2009 while I was recruiting full-time.

For a moment, it felt like maybe, just maybe, we were finding our way.

Alice seemed to be thriving at the firehouse. She introduced me to Ben, the fire chief. Charismatic, confident, warm, the kind of guy who smiled with his whole face and always asked how I was doing.

We needed a medic on the SWAT team, and Ben looked like the perfect fit: professional, competent, and trustworthy.
I vouched for him.
He joined the team.
We trained together.
I let him into our circle.

I let my guard down.

That fall, I got a small role in a low-budget movie filming in the county. It wasn't much, but it paid, and more than that, it was something for me. Something fun. Something selfish. I hadn't done that in years.

The only downside? The shoot landed on Alice's birthday.

I offered to celebrate another night. She told me not to worry, she had plans with friends from the firehouse.

I stayed on set until late. When I finally called her, she didn't answer. When she did, she said they were heading over to Ben's brother Joe's place to continue the night.

Something about it didn't sit right.

I offered to pick her up; she'd been drinking. She brushed it off.

I went anyway.

When I arrived, the door didn't open. I knocked. Again. And again.

Finally, Joe cracked the door and stepped outside.

"She's not here," he said, blocking the entry.

"I just talked to her," I said. **"I know she's here."**

Eventually, Alice stumbled out. She was drunk. Dismissive. She laughed it off like I was being paranoid.

And for the hundredth time, I swallowed the unease and drove her home in silence. But I knew.

Something had shifted.

The Confirmation

Four months later, my suspicions became certainty.

On February 3, 2013, Ben's wife called me.

She'd caught them together, Alice and Ben. She told me it had been going on for months.

And she confirmed what I feared most:

The night of Alice's birthday, while I was on set, trying to build something for myself, Alice was sleeping with Ben. At Joe's house.

Every late-night shift. Every "friend from the firehouse." Every unexplained deflection.

The dam broke. I confronted Alice. She didn't flinch.

She told me she wanted a divorce. No apology. No remorse.

Just a flat declaration:

"I'm done."

And I was done too.

I packed a bag. Grabbed my gear. Called a buddy and asked to crash on his couch.

I didn't have a plan. I didn't have money. And for the first time in years, I didn't have hope.

The kids were everything to me.

They were the reason I'd survived the worst of Afghanistan and Iraq. The only reason I never pulled the trigger when the pressure got too high.

And now, I was at risk of losing them.

Alice said she wanted to keep all the kids together.

What she meant was she wanted my kids, Jakub and Zoe, to stay and help raise hers.

That wasn't going to happen. I wasn't abandoning them again.

The betrayal was brutal. But what made it worse was how quickly Ben moved in.

Three days.

That's all it took for him to be sleeping in my bed, eating at my table, while I was sleeping on a friend's couch. I was humiliated. I was furious. Really furious.

The Fall

I started therapy again. I laid it all out, the war, the betrayal, the rage, the sleepless nights. I told the therapist I didn't trust myself anymore.

She asked me if I could hurt Alice.

I said something stupid. Something raw.

"I could shoot her."

It wasn't a threat. It was a cry for help.

But therapists don't gamble. She reported it.

I was given a choice: Voluntarily commit to a psychiatric hospital, or be court-ordered.

I knew what a court order meant:

Loss of rights.

Career.

Reputation.

So I checked myself in.

A week of fluorescent lights, group therapy circles, hollow conversations.

I told them what they needed to hear. Played the part. Nodded at the right times. Got discharged.

But it wasn't over.

When I got out, a state trooper was waiting.

Protective order. No contact with Alice.

No returning home.

But the divorce court had issued a separate order:

Four days to retrieve my belongings from the house.

The first three days, I did what I could: uniforms, keepsakes, essentials.

On the fourth day, Alice refused to leave.

I called. Asked her to leave my things on the porch.

She said no.

I called the Sheriff's Department, my own department, to request a deputy stand by.

They said no. Claimed they didn't do standbys.

That was a lie. I'd done myself plenty.

Eventually, I saw her car pull away. I went to the house.

My key didn't work. She'd changed the locks. Through the window, I saw my belongings in trash bags.

I called again.

No answer. I snapped. kicked in the side door. Grabbed my gear. Loaded the car.

Trying to avoid confusion, I called dispatch:

"This isn't a burglary. It's me, retrieving items under court order."

They sent a supervisor.

Then a trooper, the same one who'd served the protective order.

He said I'd violated it. I explained the court's conflicting order.

He didn't care.

I was arrested.

For breaking into my own house.

Charged with Criminal Mischief and Invasion of Privacy.

Suspended from the department.

My career.

My reputation.

My family.

Gone.

And I had no one to blame but myself.

The following weeks were a blur of shame, bourbon, and suicidal thoughts.
I sat alone, bottle in hand, gun on the table, wondering if anyone would miss me.

And then the phone rang.

The Call:

It was SFC Van Huffel.

The same man I refused to betray. The only one who'd seen me at my lowest and stayed.

"There's a recruiting spot up here in Michigan," he said. **"You need a fresh start. I can't promise it'll be easy, but it's a way out. Think about it."**

That call saved my life.

Leadership Debrief: Lessons from Rock Bottom

- **Pain doesn't disqualify you from leading; it refines you.** The worst seasons of your life may become your greatest teachers.
- **Don't confuse control with strength.** Kicking in a door feels powerful, but true strength is choosing discipline when you have every reason not to.
- **When everything falls apart, pay attention.** Rock bottom isn't the end. It's the place you decide who you'll be next.
- **Systems aren't always fair.** You can't always control outcomes, but you can control your response.
- **There's a cost to unresolved trauma.** You can't outrun war, betrayal, and burnout. Get help before it breaks you.

I wasn't the man I wanted to be. I was angry. Broken.

Ashamed, but I wasn't finished.

That call from Van Huffel wasn't just about a job.

It was a lifeline. A second chance.

And when no one else believed in me, He did.

And that was all I needed… to try again. I would **lead anyway**.

Chapter 19
The Rebuild

The phone call didn't just come at the right time; it came at the last possible moment.

I was sitting in a dark room, the air thick with silence, broken only by the ticking of a cheap wall clock. A half-empty bottle of bourbon sat beside my service pistol on the nightstand. The room smelled like stale liquor and surrender. I hadn't eaten in a day. Hadn't slept in two. My thoughts had turned inward and ugly, and I found myself staring into the void, asking questions that had no good answers.

The kind of pain I felt doesn't roar. It whispers. It taps your shoulder with soft, icy fingers, telling you that everything you've done, everything you've become, has amounted to nothing. That the world would move on more easily without you. That maybe, just maybe, your kids would be better off.

And if you sit in that lie long enough, you start to believe it.

That's where I was, right on the edge, when the phone rang.

SFC James Van Huffel.

His name flashed across the screen like a spotlight cutting through fog. He was a friend. A teammate. A man who had stood with me in better times and never wavered in worse. I hesitated. Answering meant confronting the shame I'd tried to bury.

But something deeper, instinct, maybe hope, made me pick up.

"Bill," he said, calm and grounded. "I don't care what happened down there. I care about what happens next. There's a recruiting position open in Michigan. It's not glamorous. But it's real. And it's yours if you want it."

I didn't say anything.

"I think you need this," he continued. "You need to be needed again. You need a mission. Pack your things. Head west. We'll figure it out."

That call didn't just interrupt the spiral.

It reversed it.

My voice cracked. "I'm dying here, Van."

"I know," he replied. No pity. Just knowing. "That's why I'm calling."

It wasn't just a job offer. It was a rescue mission. A last chance. A hand reaching down into a pit I didn't know how to climb out of.

I said yes.

Leaving the Sheriff's Department didn't bring sadness. The writing was already on the wall. It was only a matter of time before I'd be fired or forced out. But this? This gave me something else, an exit with dignity, with purpose, and most importantly: with hope.

I grabbed what little we had, loaded up Zoe and Jakub, and headed west.

Not north. West. To a new life.

We landed in a modest, older house on the south side of South Bend. The walls needed paint. The roof had seen better days.

But none of that mattered. It was ours. It was safe. It was the first piece of normal I had offered my kids in years.

Zoe and Jakub had been through hell, different schools, temporary homes, whispers in the hallway. A father who was more shadow than shelter.

I had failed them in so many ways.

Now, I had a chance to rebuild something that could last.

Mission: Rebuild

I threw myself into recruiting like my life depended on it, because it did.

Ten-, twelve-hour days.

Weekends. Early mornings. Late nights. Not because someone told me to. Because I had something to prove. I needed to know I could still matter. That I could still contribute. That I wasn't just a man defined by the worst year of his life.

They gave me the hardest areas. The forgotten zip codes. The places nobody else wanted.

I didn't care. I didn't need easy. I needed real. I needed redemption through effort.

I went to every school. Met every counselor. Built relationships with every community leader who would listen.

I showed up. I listened.

I didn't just talk benefits, I talked life. Purpose. Options.

I didn't recruit numbers. I recruited people.

Each applicant got the truth, the good, the bad, and the brutally honest. And I asked every single one of them the same question I had once asked myself:

"What are you going to do when you're done serving?"

Then I helped them build a plan for that answer.

Slowly, my world began to stabilize.

By 2014, I wasn't just surviving. I was performing.

And with that stability came the courage to try again.

To believe, for the first time in a long time, that maybe I could build something lasting with someone.

But I wasn't going to repeat the same mistakes.

This time, I had standards.

She needed to be close to my age. No desire for more kids. Emotionally healthy.

Financially stable. No rescue missions. No chaos.

I'd had enough of both.

I went on a few dates. Kind women. Smart women. But none that fit.

And I was okay with that. For once, I wasn't rushing. I wasn't desperate. I was protecting what I had rebuilt.

Then Came Lynn

In January 2015, I got a message online. Five simple words:

"Thank you for your service."

It was common enough. But something about it felt sincere. Different.

I replied.

"Thank you. My name is Bill."

Her name was Lynn. She was a nurse. Twice divorced. Two kids. No plans for more.

She was living in her sister's basement, but she wasn't stuck. She had goals.

Direction.
Forward motion.

And a calm, quiet strength that drew me in.

We met for coffee. She chose the place. She set the tone.

And I loved that.

Our conversation wasn't flirty. It was raw. Honest. Real.

We talked about trauma. Failure. Divorce Kids. Finances.

All the mess. No filters.

We stayed until the café lights dimmed.

When I walked her to her car, I went for the safe hug.

She kissed me. A test. I passed. From that night forward, she became a steadying force.

Not someone who tried to fix me.

Someone who stood beside me while I fixed myself.

She came with me to court. Listened to my fears. Helped me face the wreckage without making me feel small.

Eventually, I was acquitted. The system cleared my name. But Lynn had already cleared the path.

I was promoted to Sergeant First Class. Re-enrolled in college. Started leading with confidence again.

And when I asked Lynn to marry me, she said yes.

We were married in May 2017. One year later, I graduated from Trine University with my bachelor's degree.

It wasn't just a new chapter. It was a new book.

We bought a home together. Merged routines. Created structure.

Jakub joined the National Guard. Then Nathan, Lynn's son, followed.

Our six children, Vivienne, Madeline, Abigail, Zoe, Jakub, and Nathan, became one team. Different bloodlines. Different stories. One roof. One family.

In 2020, I was promoted to Master Sergeant. Earned a Master's degree from Michigan State. Then an MBA from Notre Dame.

But the degrees weren't the reward.

The peace was.

Leadership Debrief: Lessons from The Rebuild

- **Redemption takes work.** You don't stumble into healing. You earn it, with sweat, with tears, with decisions nobody sees.
- **Boundaries are leadership.** Saying *no* to chaos is saying *yes* to stability, for yourself and those you lead.
- **Transparency builds trust.** Vulnerability isn't weakness; it's the soil where real connection grows.
- **Your past doesn't define your potential.** Scars prove you survived. They're not signs you're broken.
- **You don't rebuild alone.** Let people in. Choose teammates. Real leaders build teams, even at home.

I stopped trying to impress. I started trying to build. Not for applause. Not for redemption. For life. For legacy. Leadership doesn't always mean standing tall in front of a crowd. Sometimes, it means standing back up when no one's watching.

And this time, I wasn't standing alone.

I didn't need to be perfect.

I just needed to show up.

Every day. With heart. With humility. And the relentless decision to **lead anyway**.

Chapter 20
Still Standing

I've been called a lot of things in my life: Soldier, Sergeant, Officer, Dad, Recruiter, Husband, Leader.

But if I had to sum it all up in one word?

Survivor.

I survived the chaos of childhood dysfunction and the shame of failure. I survived war. I survived betrayal. I survived *myself.* I made more mistakes than I can count, but I also kept getting back up.

That's the part people miss when they talk about "resilience." It's not about bouncing back like a rubber band. It's about dragging yourself forward, some days on bloody knees and broken pride, and choosing to show up again, even when every part of you wants to disappear.

This book wasn't written to make me look good. It was written to tell the truth. The messy, raw, embarrassing truth.

Because too many people see leadership as a TED Talk, a LinkedIn post, or a title on a door. Something polished. Something perfect.

It's not.

Leadership is being the one who says, *"I'll take care of it,"* even when no one else will. Leadership is stepping into the breach, again and again, for people who may never even say thank you. It's choosing character over comfort. Truth over image. Purpose over popularity.

It's apologizing when you mess it up. Owning it. And trusting that your story's not over just because you wrecked a few chapters.

So if you're reading this and you've fallen *hard*, I need you to hear me:

You are not disqualified. You are not broken beyond repair. And you are sure as hell not done.

The world doesn't need more perfect people. It needs more *real* people.

People who are willing to **lead anyway**, through the doubt, through the scars, through the chaos.

People like you.

You see, leadership isn't found in corner offices or Instagram bios. It's found in the quiet choices no one sees. Waking up when you don't feel like it. Going to work when you'd rather quit. Having the hard conversation.

Raising your hand when the easy thing is to lower your head. Showing up for your kids when your heart is broken.

Leadership isn't always loud. Sometimes, it's a whisper that says:

"Try again."

And that's what I did. Again. And again. And again.

And here I am, *still standing*.

With six kids. A third marriage that finally feels like home. Degrees on the wall that don't define me, but reflect the fight. A military retirement within reach. And a new mission burning inside me like a torch:

To help others find their footing, own their scars, and lead from wherever they are.

I've learned that you don't need a rank to lead.
You don't need a title to matter.

You just need to show up.

Even when it's hard. Especially when it's hard.

Because if someone like me, flawed, fallen, and fired, can rebuild a life worth living…

Then so can you.

And if you're thinking, *"But I'm not strong enough,"*, you're wrong. Because strength isn't about never breaking. It's about refusing to stay broken.

I've walked through hell twice. I've faced courts, commanders, and custody battles. I've slept in empty houses and sat in darker rooms. I've had my name dragged through the mud. I've been forgotten. Pitied. Feared. Written off.

But I'm still here.

Why?

Because I refused to let failure be the last word.

Every scar I carry, I earned. But I also earned the right to tell the story of what came *next*.

That's what this book is.

Not a highlight reel, A survival guide.

A roadmap for rebuilding.

And if I could boil everything I've learned into one sentence, it's this:

You don't have to be perfect to lead; you just have to keep showing up with purpose.

That's it.

You don't need a five-year plan.

You don't need permission. You don't need to wait until you feel "ready."

You just need to start.

Take one small step today toward the life you want to lead.

Have the conversation. Make the call. Get back in the gym.

Apologize.

Apply.

Pray.

Pack up. Speak up.

Let go.

Do *one* thing that your future self will thank you for.

And if you don't know where to start, start here:

Look in the mirror and say, **"I'm not done."**

Say it until you believe it.

Say it until you *become* it.

Because you aren't done.

You're just getting started.

Leadership Debrief: Final Dispatch

- **Failure doesn't disqualify you. Quitting on yourself does.** You can fall and still move forward. Just don't stop trying.
- **The most powerful leadership comes from lived experience, not polished credentials.** Your mess may be your ministry. Your pain might be your platform.

- **Redemption requires action.** It's not about waiting for forgiveness; it's about changing what you do *today*.
- **Boundaries are leadership.** Know what you'll allow, what you won't tolerate, and what you're working toward. Protect your peace like it's your purpose.
- **You don't lead because you're the strongest.** You lead because you remember what it's like to be weak, and you choose to rise anyway.
- **You don't have to fix everything.** You just have to be the one willing to face it. Courage doesn't come from clarity. It comes from commitment.

To the Reader

This is your call to action.

Don't just *read* this book. Use it.

If you're stuck, get up. If you're leading, lead better. If you're healing, keep going.

You don't need permission to lead. You don't need to wait to be chosen.

You already are.

So take the wisdom here, earned the hard way, and go build something that lasts.

Lead your family.

Lead your team.

Lead your life.

Lead anyway.

Because the world isn't changed by perfect people.

It's changed by survivors who refuse to stay down.

It's changed by people like you.

Author's Final Word: From One Survivor to Another

If you're still with me, still reading, still breathing, still searching—thank you.

This wasn't an easy book to write. It probably wasn't an easy book to read.

But that's the point.

This isn't a collection of success stories dressed up in motivational quotes. This is blood-on-the-page truth. And if you saw yourself in any of these chapters, any of the breakdowns, battles, or breakthroughs, then know this:

You are not alone.

I wrote this for you. For the person who's still standing when they have every reason not to be. For the one holding it together with duct tape and prayer. For the leader who doubts they're enough. For the dad who feels like he's blown it. For the fighter who's still searching for purpose.

I don't know where life has taken you, or what it's taken from you, but I do know this:

If you're still standing, you're still in the fight.

And you don't need anyone's permission to begin again.

You don't have to wait for someone to rescue you. You don't have to wait for the pain to disappear. You don't have to wait until you feel "worthy."

You just have to *move*.

That's what survivors do.

We move forward, even when it hurts. We build again, even when the rubble's still warm. We lead, not because we have all the answers, but because we've lived through the questions.

And we keep showing up.

So let me say what I wish someone had said to me in the darkest moments:

You are not too far gone. You are not beyond repair. You are not the worst thing you've ever done, or the worst thing that's ever been done to you.

You are a survivor.

And if you're willing to lead with your scars, to step forward with open hands and a wide-open heart, then you'll do more than survive.

You'll lead others to life.

That's the gift of pain transformed. That's the power of purpose rediscovered.

So here's your final charge:

Don't waste the wreckage.

Use it.

Build with it.

Teach with it.

Heal with it.

And when people ask how you made it through, tell them the truth:

"I decided to get up *again.*"

Lead anyway,

Bill Long

About The Author

William Long Jr. is a career leader, veteran, and educator whose life has been shaped by service, responsibility, and the hard lessons learned when things go wrong before they go right.

He has spent nearly three decades leading in environments where decisions carry real consequences, from combat deployments and humanitarian missions overseas to law enforcement, military recruiting, and training leaders at scale. Across every role, his leadership philosophy has remained consistent: leadership is not about perfection; it is about presence.

William has served as a Soldier in Afghanistan and Iraq, a SWAT officer, and a senior military recruiting and retention leader responsible for developing and mentoring hundreds of leaders. His work has spanned crisis response, training design, performance improvement, and organizational leadership. He is the author of Mission Ready, a leadership and training guide adopted within military environments, and Lead Anyway is his most personal work to date.

Beyond uniforms and titles, William is a husband, father, and lifelong student of leadership. He holds an Executive MBA from the University of Notre Dame and is currently pursuing a doctorate in Leadership and Learning in Organizations at Vanderbilt University. His writing draws from lived experience, academic study, and the belief that the most meaningful leadership lessons are forged in struggle, not the spotlight.

William lives with his family in the Midwest. When he is not writing or teaching, he remains committed to mentoring, training, and helping others find clarity and resilience in difficult seasons of life.

www.ingramcontent.com/pod-product-compliance
Lightning Source LLC
LaVergne TN
LVHW022108200926
848481LV00003B/1102
* 9 7 9 8 2 9 5 5 5 6 1 7 3 *